THE SOCIAL AND CULTURAL LIFE OF THE 1920s

Edited by **RONALD L. DAVIS**
Southern Methodist University

HOLT RINEHART AND WINSTON, INC.
New York • Chicago • San Francisco • Atlanta
Dallas • Montreal • Toronto • London • Sydney

Cover Illustration: *Life* magazine cover, October 28,
1926. *(The Granger Collection)*

WITHDRAWN

THE SOCIAL AND CULTURAL LIFE
OF THE 1920s

**Books are to be returned on or before
the last date below.**

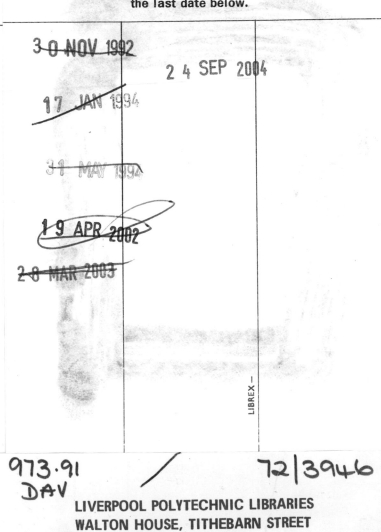

3 0 NOV 1992

2 4 SEP 2004

17 JAN 1994

3 1 MAY 1994

1 9 APR 2002

2 8 MAR 2003

LIBREX —

CONTENTS

page 107

Ziegfield Follies girls frolicking at Brighton Beach, 1923. *(The Bettmann Archive)*

INTRODUCTION

Few decades of the recent American past have evoked more widespread fascination than the 1920s. Hollywood films such as *Pete Kelly's Blues, Some Like It Hot,* and *Thoroughly Modern Millie* and weekly television series like *The Untouchables* have etched in the popular mind the stereotype of the Roaring Twenties—reputedly a wild, tumultuous era whose rebellious, hyperthyroid youth spent themselves on rotgut booze, speakeasy jazz, and rumbleseat sex, punctuated by the blast of the sawed-off shotgun and the squeal of the get-away car. Writers of the period have supported the image by focusing on the trivia of the decade, creating a collage of flivvers, flappers, pockmarked bootleggers, flagpole sitters, prohibition agents, celluloid lovers, and sophomoric spokesmen of Freudian psychology. The Twenties have variously been termed the "Era of Wonderful Nonsense," "The Aspirin Age," "The Lawless Decade," "The Passionate Years," and most often, "The Jazz Age" by chroniclers who either regard the period as an adolescent spree or with a regret approximating that of a bad hangover. To judge from some reports, Americans in the 1920s did little more than make millions on the stock market, dance the Black Bottom and Charleston, wear raccoon coats, carry hip flasks, and dodge gangsters' bullets.

In part this emphasis on the frivolity and violence of the 1920s results from the history of the period having largely been written by journalists and popularizers rather than by professional scholars. Frederick Lewis Allen's *Only Yesterday* (1931) more than any other single volume set the tone for interpretation of the social and cultural history of the decade. While Allen's book is superlative in many respects, showing remarkable insight in synthesizing yesterday's headlines, the author's journalistic penchant for emphasizing the glamorous aspects of the period and his tendency toward overgeneralization temper his worth as an historian. For Allen the 1920s marked the beginning of a new era in American thought which shelved traditional values and witnessed the rise of a happy hedonism, blind cynicism, and an irresponsible materialism. *Only Yesterday* envisions a people rising out of the shambles of World War I, an age when "everything seemed meaningless and unimportant." The Wilsonian bubble of idealism had burst, and Americans drifted toward some vague redefinition of self-identity, disillusioned and spiritually exhausted. The nation's youth reveled in a "revolu-

1

tion in manners and morals" largely because they had little else to do and no more important life goal.

At the same time Allen was too astute not to recognize that underneath the period's superficial froth ran currents deeper and more portentous. With the ideological derailment following the war and the resulting collapse of established values, intellectuals revolted against the puritanical, materialistic absolutism of American civilization, deploring its repressive insistence on conformity. Instead they extolled a glorified individual freedom, an independent search for meaning. For some the quest led to a cynicism bordering on nihilism, for others toward at least a partial acceptance of the world as absurd, for many more toward a romantic probing of emotion, illusion, other social patterns, and the exotic, yet with no real hope of finding eternal answers. So repulsive was mechanical, unfeeling industrial America to the "lost generation" that they abandoned the esthetic desert they perceived as their own country in favor of European oases of culture, particularly Paris.

For the expatriates the United States, with its sex taboos and blatant commercialism, represented a social fabric that for the individual was emotionally smothering and esthetically poisoned. The American exiles in Europe, John W. Aldridge points out, were looking for a new meaning, in many cases embracing a religion of art. The impulse toward exile, like the impulse toward the adoration of art, emerged from their need to sustain the emotions aroused in them by the war, to continue the incessant movement, the constant search for excitement, and to seek out another faith to replace the one lost during the war.

The steady rise of the American city after the Civil War and the sudden emergence of the United States as a world leader brought to the surface and amplified tensions that had been mounting in the country since the industrial phalanx first threatened invasion of the pastoral village. By the beginning of the twentieth century the dominion of rural, small-town America was not only being usurped by the city, but also traditional economic, political, social, and moral patterns were being challenged by the crystallization of an urban viewpoint. The rise of the city upset class relationships and produced, for the first time in this country, a defined body of full-time intellectuals. As attitudes changed, conservative sanctuaries of American thought grew increasingly alarmed, the anxieties swelling by the 1920s into pockets of neuroses. Most of all, however, traditional America was disturbed by the mores of the metropolis, which represented all that prewar America feared most—Wall Street, Europe, political radicalism, religious skepticism, sophistication, intellectual arrogance.

The reaction attempted not simply to preserve the rural character of American life, but in crucial areas to turn the clock back and restore cherished ideals of the nineteenth century. Manifesting in part the frenzied efforts to rekindle beleaguered absolutes, the United States in the decade after 1915 experienced the revival of the Ku Klux Klan, the Red Scare, the enactment of prohibition, an intensification of the fundamentalist crusade, militant racism, the selection of William H. Hays to supervise movie censorship, and an expanded restatement of American materialism, broadened to encompass the vast technological advances of the past half century. Emerging as a symbol of this enlarged materialism was Henry Ford, whose mass-produced automobile became for many one of the immediate tokens of national progress. Yet at the same time, Ford championed the spiritual standards of rural America, creating in Greenfield Village a replica of a small nineteenth-century town, complete with gravel roads, gas lights, horse-drawn vehicles, and an old-fashioned country store. The manufacturer deplored modern dancing, delighted in folk tunes like "Arkansas Traveler," and subsidized the printing and distribution of selections from the time-honored *McGuffey Reader*. Ford, who had begun tinkering with machines to escape the drudgery of farm work, sought valiantly to enshrine the simplicity of yesterday, at a moment when his assembly line was making the tranquility of the rural ideal increasingly obsolete.

As the disparity in American values multiplied, the warring factions tended to polarize into extremes. At times the conflicts between representatives of the traditional element and heralds of the new viewpoint became as bitter as they were extensive. The hysterical nature of the reactionary radical is effectively illustrated both by the fundamentalist crusade and the prohibition experiment, since in each instance a pugnacious determination to strengthen a dying viewpoint is clearly defined. The basic cause of the fundamentalist controversy as explained by Norman F. Furniss was "the incompatibility of the nineteenth-century orthodoxy cherished by many humble Americans with the progress made in science and theology since the Civil War." Conservatives awoke to find their authoritative faith besieged from two directions. Modernism, stemming from higher criticism, rejected outmoded concepts of the Scriptures, while the theory of evolution directly challenged the Bible's affirmation of man's fiat creation. For the fundamentalists the acceptance of modernism and evolution clearly reflected the growing contamination of a society drifting from holy precepts toward a mirage of sophistication. To abate the sacrilege, stalwarts would ultimately attempt to write their dogma into law, thereby fortifying past absolutes from urban profanity.

The prohibition movement, as Andrew Sinclair demonstrates, was no less emotional in temper, and its leaders were also inclined toward extremism. Although there were reasonable economic, medical, and moral reasons for supporting prohibition, the drys themselves emphasized mainly irrational arguments. "There was an element of sadism and undue persecution in the drys' legislative pursuit of the sinner," Sinclair insists, just as in the flogging of bootleggers and prostitutes by the Ku Klux Klan.

The conservative entrenchment doubtlessly served to reinforce the intellectuals' reservations about American standards and to dilate the restlessness of sophisticated youth, encouraging the vanguard of each group toward hyperbole. The question, however, is not so much whether or not there was extremism in the United States during the 1920s, for surely the conflict between rural and urban values that had been surfacing in the country since the Civil War had reached a head during the years after World War I. The problem rather concerns the extent to which American life and thought were affected by the struggle and the degree to which the resulting tension permeated the ranks of American society. In what measure did either the discontent of the youth or the intellectual merit the term "revolt"? Was the intensity of either, in numbers or ideology, sufficient to justify repeated overstatement? How much did the conservative assaults reflect bona fide attitudes of the American public? In what areas did they simply represent the well-organized endeavors of an aggressive minority?

In the ferment of rebellion and reaction of the decade, the search for meaning and individualism took on various important dimensions. Certainly the nineteenth-century emphasis on material success continued into the 1920s as a fundamental folk ideal, often sharpened by technological progress and high-powered advertising. The mass mind remained dedicated to a religion of work, James Prothro demonstrates, while business leaders took "unashamed pride with Babbitt in material accomplishment." During what Prothro calls the "Dollar Decade," the National Association of Manufacturers and the Chamber of Commerce came to view material gain as the major point of focus for man's aspirations and energies. Sickened by such sentiments, the expatriates fled to Paris, as much to escape the shackles of American materialism as to liberate themselves from Puritan morals. Likewise many of the bohemians, as Caroline Ware discusses, professed a disregard for values and prestige based either on income or conspicuous spending, substituting instead some type of spiritual values and a tolerance for unconventional behavior even when their own conduct was more restrained.

The high regard for art displayed both by the bohemians and the expatriates suggests in part their questioning of industrial materialism, in marked "contrast to the Babbitt-ridden communities from which they had escaped." Inferred also is a shift in the concept of personal worth, away from traditional "rugged individualism" toward an esthetic expression of self. The vast changes taking place in the American experience since the Civil War made increasingly difficult the preservation of an individualism rooted in the frontier, and the closing of the West was paralleled by a growing restlessness. As urbanization continued in the early twentieth century and as the industrial complex appeared steadily more confining, Americans generally—rather than alienating themselves from society—demonstrated a desire to transfer the dreams of yesterday, the optimism of the frontier, to modern machinery.

Much of the aimless search for meaning and self-fulfillment in the 1920s may perhaps have resulted from an anxious effort to cling to a frontier orientation, as Americans partially sublimated their pioneering aggressions in golf, spectator

sports, summer vacations, lodge night, marathon dancing, and sensational jour-
nalism—in a sense looking for a new frontier. Indeed the desire for new frontiers
was strong with Americans of the 1920s, at times bordering on obsession. Lindbergh's flight in 1927 serves as a classic example, indicating too the ambivalence
of the American mind. The transatlantic challenge was conquered by a shy mid-
westerner who became the embodiment of pioneer daring and conventional virtue. Lindbergh gave the American people a symbol of their fundamental ideals
at a time when it was feared these attitudes were being deserted. The aviator
represented the old-style hero, courageous and self-reliant, who had employed
machine technology to modernize frontier individualism. The popular reaction
against the structure of a mechanized society, Ward speculates, "probably led to
the nostalgic image of Lindbergh as a remnant of a past when romance was possible for the individual, when life held novelty and society was variegated rather
than uniform." At the same time his transatlantic flight glorified an advanced
development of urban, industrialized society, heralding for many a day when the
machine would lead to some new paradise. Lindbergh therefore served both as
a link to the past and a bridge to the future.

Yet Franz Alexander insists that the fixation with frontier ideals caused
Americans in the face of a consolidating society to withdraw into fantasy—a more
dangerous retreat than mere daydreaming. The frontier disregard for law and
order, the notion of each man's taking justice into his own hands became per-
verted into crime and violence, with the "tough guy" becoming something of a
public hero. Widespread neurosis was another evidence of the ideological lag,
Alexander feels, as the worship of individual success continued in an industrial
society drawing increasingly interdependent.

For others a technological future, no matter how dependent on the individual, was a chimeric projection of man's potential. What was to become of human
dignity, personal nobility, beauty, and emotion? For some the industrial web
stifled the individual, humiliated him, and isolated him spiritually from his fellow man. Artists and intellectuals of the 1920s frequently voiced the desire to
avoid social involvement, to build for themselves their own world based on personalized values. While nineteenth-century realism continued in the arts, the
prosperity of the 1920s and the lack of an imminent national calamity allowed
for much experimentation. Feeling himself less an organic part of society than
before and less concerned with combating social evils, the artist was freer to move
toward abstraction and, if he chose, devote himself more fully to pure estheticism.
Although a cultural ferment preceded the United States' entry into World War I,
the 1920s saw an interest in the arts unprecedented in the nation's past.

The reactionary attack on modernism in the arts, however, was no less vehe-
ment, although less far-reaching, than that against free thought in morals and
religion. The abstract and cubist painters of the 1920s may have been much in the
limelight, but the lion's share of the furor was negative. Conventional art critics

even suggested that the ultimate goal of these artists was to overturn morality and Christianity. Considerably more heated was the controversy over jazz, the music from New Orleans viewed among conservatives as a stimulant to the downfall of the youth and possibly a threat to civilization itself. The social and moral implications, Neil Leonard observes, "made the jazz controversy part of the bitter conflict between the relative norms which were gaining currency and traditional, absolute values." The unstructured, emotional qualities of jazz were considered enemies both to academic music and a well-ordered society. The brothel origins of the music offended the middle-class sense of propriety, as did its later association with vice. The heavy Negro influence was looked upon with suspicion by an Anglo-Saxon majority, reflecting the racial tensions of the period. The strongest opposition, Leonard maintains, came from those whose status related most closely to conventional values. As long as such inflexible esthetic standards delineated American tastes, what chances did an artistic revolution have for success? How was a dynamic American culture to emerge?

While modernism in painting met profuse opposition, the break with formalism begun before World War I continued its ferment in the 1920s, though with less energy than in the preceding decade. David A. Shannon indicates in his survey of the art of the 1920's that a broader segment of American society, largely because of the prosperity of the period, began purchasing paintings other than portraits for their homes. Sixty new museums were established during the decade, although Shannon concludes that most Americans still lived out their lives without ever viewing a great work of art. Artists continued to experiment with abstraction and cubism, announced to the New York public by the explosive Armory Show of 1913, but in most instances their techniques retreated toward the traditional. Essentially the decade represented a digestive period for the modern painter in the United States. To what extent was the artist limited by his society? How does the opposition to modern painting compare with the traditionalists' opposition to jazz?

The DeVoto-Hoffman dialogue regarding the merits of the literature of the 1920s deepens the argument over the nature of art and the relationship between the artist and society. Major writers of the decade often concerned themselves more with individual experience than with social problems, expressing the need for private experimentation both in life and art. In Bernard DeVoto's opinion these writers were irresponsible, dissolute adolescents who became trapped in a pointless negativism. Frederick J. Hoffman, on the contrary, takes their literary achievements seriously, finding the postwar writers more innocent than lost. True, they were receptive to practically every new influence that came along, Hoffman admits, but they rebelled and explored in order to rebuild. In the process "they formulated in several brilliant ways the most important of all symbolic figurations of our century—that of isolation, of the single, dispossessed soul whose life needs to be re-established in terms specifically new and unencumbered."

The 1920s have been judged both as a "golden age" and as a "hollow time between wars." The years have been seen as frivolous and roaring, at the same time bathed in tragedy and despair. One school of American historians has viewed the period as bequeathing virtually nothing of permanent value and much that was troublesome to future generations. Another has found the decade amazingly vital, filled with significant change, perhaps representing the formative years of modern American society.

For Bruce Catton, "The decade of the nineteen twenties was at one and the same time the gaudiest, the saddest, and the most misinterpreted era in modern American history." For William Leuchtenburg, "It was a time of paradoxes: an age of conformity and of liberation, of the persistence of rural values and the triumph of the city, of isolationism and new internationalist ventures, of laissez faire but also of government intervention, of competition and of merger, of despair and of joyous abandon." For Roderick Nash, "The decade after the war was a time of heightened anxiety when intellectual guideposts were sorely needed and diligently sought. Many clung tightly to the familiar moorings of traditional custom and value. Others actively sought new ways of understanding and ordering their existence. Americans from 1917 to 1930 constituted a *nervous* generation, groping for what certainty they could find."

Frederick Lewis Allen's insistence that a "first-class revolt against the accepted American order" took place among the postwar youth has been embellished time and again by writers on the period. Yet revisionists like Roderick Nash argue that this long-accepted picture of flaming nonconformity has been sharply overdrawn. How much of the "revolution in manners and morals" was merely a fad? How much of it was manufactured by the press? Did it really indicate a breakdown of the family, a rejection of social controls, or the liberation of the youth? After all, even F. Scott Fitzgerald admitted in 1931 that the "jazz age" concept he had created earlier was limited to the "upper tenth of [the] nation." Roderick Nash is convinced that "revolutionary and bizarre" behavior in the 1920s has been exaggerated. "In fact," Nash concludes, "popular thought in these years was remarkably conservative. Beneath the eye-catching outward iconoclasm, the symbolic revolt, was a thick layer of respect for time-honored American ways, means, and rationales."

Similarly, the cynicism and alienation of the "lost generation" has recently been called into question. Clearly the intellectual insurgents cannot be taken as typical even of progressive American thought during the Twenties, and the memoirs of a select circle of literati may well have distorted the impression of the decade. "Intellectuals were by no means unanimous in professing the disillusionment of the expatriates, bohemians, and satirists," Nash cautions. "For a great many thoughtful Americans World War I did not mean intellectual derailment. The threads of continuity in the history of ideas are visible across the war years, as they are across most so-called watersheds." The despair of the intelligentsia has also been challenged by other recent historians, who insist that the generation of the 1920s accepted a far greater intellectual heritage from the "Gilded Age" than it generally cared to admit. How extensive, one must ask, was the rejection or even the questioning of traditional American concepts? To what degree did intellectual leaders of the period redefine American values? Can the argument that the 1920s witnessed the shaping of modern thought be supported?

While F. Scott Fitzgerald, Ernest Hemingway, and Gertrude Stein may be considered today among the great names of American letters, their works did not establish themselves as national best-sellers in the 1920s. Instead the reading public preferred Gene Stratton-Porter, Zane Grey, and Harold Bell Wright. "Frontier and rural patterns of thought and action dominated the popular novels," Nash observes. "Their plots and protagonists operated according to time-honored standards of competition, loyalty, and rugged individualism." While the 1920s may justly constitute on the one hand the "gaudiest spree in history," much of the routine of American life nevertheless perservered, as basic attitudes from the previous century endured. "The people of the 1920s really behaved about the way the people of all other decades have behaved," Catton declares. Most Americans remained "serious, hard-working people who did their best to earn a living, bring up their children, live decently by the best light they had, and lay away a few dollars for their old age."

Despite the democratic political leaning of the United States, the country's social attitudes until the twentieth century had largely been set by a small group of politicians, lawyers, preachers, educators, and later by the parvenu wealth spawned by post-Civil War industrialism. From 1920 on, the mass tastes became increasingly important in popular culture and, shortly, in political and economic considerations. The creative personality of the 1920's often felt trapped between an "old society" which limited free expression and a "big society" which seemed to have no sense of style at all. "Ironically," Leuchtenburg insists, "at the very time when intellectuals were complaining that art could not flourish in America, art burgeoned as it rarely, perhaps never, had before." If this observation is accurate, how may the paradox be explained? What intellectual forces lay beneath the period's surface froth? Was it an empty, drifting interlude of disintegration between two reform eras, or a vigorous time of experimentation?

Whether the Twenties in America are most judiciously characterized as a period of ballyhoo, serious questioning, deepened intellectual rebellion, artistic flowering, conservative resistance, transition, or nervous tension is a problem historians continue to debate. The issues are multifaceted, the shadings as varied as the spectrum of society and the debate made all the more germane by perceptible similarities to our own time.

In the reprinted selections footnotes appearing in the original sources have in general been omitted unless they contribute to the argument or better understanding of the selection.

FREDERICK LEWIS ALLEN (1890–1954) was
educated at Harvard, worked two years as assistant
editor of the *Atlantic Monthly,* and at the time of the
publication of *Only Yesterday* (1931) was assistant editor
of *Harper's Magazine.* From 1941 until 1953 he served
as editor of *Harper's,* although he continued to write
fascinating accounts of contemporary American
history, notably *Since Yesterday* (1940) and *The Big
Change* (1952). His vivid portrait of the flaming youth
of the 1920s set the pace for later histories of the
decade. Was the "revolution" in morals limited to the
wealthy and the young? How much of the "revolt"
was a fad? How much was created by a sensationalist
press?*

Frederick Lewis Allen

The Moral Rebellion

A first-class revolt against the accepted American order was certainly taking place during those early years of the Post-war Decade, but it was one with which Nikolai Lenin had nothing whatever to do. The shock troops of the rebellion were not alien agitators, but the sons and daughters of well-to-do American families, who knew little about Bolshevism and cared distinctly less, and their defiance was expressed not in obscure radical publications or in soap-box speeches, but right across the family breakfast table into the horrified ears of conservative fathers and mothers. Men and women were still shivering at the Red Menace when they awoke to the no less alarming Problem of the Younger Generation, and realized that if the Constitution were not in danger, the moral code of the country certainly was.

This code, as it currently concerned young people, might have been roughly summarized as follows: Women were the guardians of morality; they were made of finer stuff than men and were expected to act accordingly. Young girls must look forward in innocence (tempered perhaps with a modicum of physiological instruction) to a romantic love match which would lead them to the altar and to living-happily-ever-after; and until the "right man" came along they must allow no male to kiss them. It was expected that some men would succumb to the temptations of sex, but only with a special class of out-lawed women; girls of respectable families were supposed to have no such temptations. Boys and girls were permitted large freedom to work and play together, with decreasing and well-nigh nominal chaperonage, but only because the code worked so well on the whole that a sort of honor system was supplanting supervision by their elders; it was taken for granted that if they had been well brought up they would never take advantage of this freedom. And although the attitude toward smoking and drinking by girls differed widely in different strata of society and different parts of the country, majority opinion held that it was morally wrong for them to smoke and could hardly imagine them showing the effects of alcohol.

The war had not long been over when cries of alarm from parents, teachers, and moral preceptors began to rend the air. For the boys and girls just growing out of adolescence were making mincemeat of this code.

The dresses that the girls—and for that matter most of the older women—were wearing seemed alarming enough. In July, 1920, a fashion-writer reported in the *New York Times* that "the American woman . . . has lifted her skirts far beyond any modest limitation," which was another way of saying that the hem was now all of nine inches above the ground. It was freely predicted that skirts would come down again in the winter of 1920–21, but instead they climbed a few scandalous inches farther. The flappers wore thin dresses, short-sleeved and occasionally (in the evening) sleeveless; some of the wilder young things rolled their stockings below their knees, revealing to the shocked eyes of virtue a fleeting glance of shin-bones and knee-cap; and many of them were visibly

using cosmetics. "The intoxication of rouge," earnestly explained Dorothy Speare in *Dancers in the Dark,* "is an insidious vintage known to more girls than mere man can ever believe." Useless for frantic parents to insist that no lady did such things; the answer was that the daughters of ladies were doing it, and even retouching their masterpieces in public. Some of them, furthermore, were abandoning their corsets. "The men won't dance with you if you wear a corset," they were quoted as saying.

The current mode in dancing created still more consternation. Not the romantic violin but the barbaric saxophone now dominated the orchestra, and to its passionate crooning and wailing the fox-trotters moved in what the editor of the Hobart College *Herald* disgustedly called a "syncopated embrace." No longer did even an inch of space separate them; they danced as if glued together, body to body, cheek to cheek. Cried the *Catholic Telegraph* of Cincinnati in righteous indignation, "The music is sensuous, the embracing of partners—the female only half dressed—is absolutely indecent; and the motions—they are such as may not be described, with any respect for propriety, in a family newspaper. Suffice it to say that there are certain houses appropriate for such dances; but those houses have been closed by law."

Supposedly "nice" girls were smoking cigarettes—openly and defiantly, if often rather awkwardly and self-consciously. They were drinking—somewhat less openly but often all too efficaciously. There were stories of daughters of the most exemplary parents getting drunk—"blotto," as their companions cheerfully put it—on the contents of the hip-flasks of the new prohibition régime, and going out joyriding with men at four in the morning. And worst of all, even at well-regulated dances they were said to retire where the eye of the most sharp-sighted chaperon could not follow, and in darkened rooms or in parked cars to engage in the unspeakable practice of petting and necking.

It was not until F. Scott Fitzgerald, who had hardly graduated from Princeton and ought to know what his generation was doing, brought out *This Side of Paradise* in April, 1920, that fathers and mothers realized fully what was afoot and how long it had been going on. Apparently the "petting party" had been current as early as 1916, and was now widely established as an indoor sport. "None of the Victorian mothers—and most of the mothers were Victorian—had any idea how casually their daughters were accustomed to be kissed," wrote Mr. Fitzgerald. ". . . Amory saw girls doing things that even in his memory would have been impossible: eating three-o'clock, after-dance suppers in impossible cafés, talking of every side of life with an air half of earnestness, half of mockery, yet with a furtive excitement that Amory considered stood for a real moral let-down. But he never realized how widespread it was until he saw the cities between New York and Chicago as one vast juvenile intrigue." The book caused a shudder to run down the national spine; did not Mr. Fitzgerald represent one of his well-nurtured heroines as brazenly confessing, "I've kissed dozens of men. I suppose I'll kiss dozens more"; and another heroine as saying to a young man (*to a young man!*), "Oh, just one person in fifty has any glimmer of what sex is. I'm hipped on Freud and all that, but it's rotten that every bit of real love in the world is ninety-nine per cent passion and one little *soupçon* of jealousy"?

It was incredible. It was abominable. What did it all mean? Was every decent standard being thrown over? Mothers read the scarlet words and wondered if they themselves "had any idea how often their daughters were accustomed to be kissed." . . . But no, this must be an exaggerated account of the misconduct of some especially depraved group. Nice girls couldn't behave like that and talk openly about passion. But in due course other books appeared to substantiate the findings of Mr. Fitzgerald: *Dancers in the Dark, The Plastic Age, Flaming Youth.* Magazine articles and newspapers reiterated the scandal. To be sure, there were plenty of communities where nice girls did not, in actual fact, "behave like that"; and even in the more sophisticated urban centers there were plenty of girls who did not. Nevertheless, there was enough fire beneath the smoke of these sensational revelations to make the Problem of the Younger Generation a topic of anxious discussion from coast to coast.

The forces of morality rallied to the attack. Dr. Francis E. Clark, the founder and president of the Christian Endeavor Society, declared that the modern "indecent dance" was "an offense against womanly purity, the very fountainhead of our family and civil life." The new style of dancing was denounced in religious journals as "impure, polluting, corrupting, debasing, destroying spirituality, increasing carnality," and the mothers and sisters and church members of the land were called upon to admonish and instruct and raise the spiritual tone of these dreadful young people. President Murphree of the University of Florida cried out with true Southern warmth, "The low-cut gowns, the rolled hose and short skirts are born of the Devil and his angels, and are carrying the present and future generations to chaos and destruction." A group of Episcopal church-women in New York, speaking with the authority of wealth and social position (for they included Mrs. J. Pierpont Morgan, Mrs. Borden Harriman, Mrs. Henry Phipps, Mrs. James Roosevelt, and Mrs. E. H. Harriman), proposed an organization to discourage fashions involving an "excess of nudity" and "improper ways of dancing." The Y. W. C. A. conducted a national campaign against immodest dress among high-school girls, supplying newspapers with printed matter carrying headlines such as "Working Girls Responsive to Modesty Appeal" and "High Heels Losing Ground Even in France." In Philadelphia a Dress Reform Committee of prominent citizens sent a questionnaire to over a thousand clergymen to ask them what would be their idea of a proper dress, and although the gentlemen of the cloth showed a distressing variety of opinion, the committee proceeded to design a "moral gown" which was endorsed by ministers of fifteen denominations. The distinguishing chatacteristics of this moral gown were that it was very loose-fitting, that the sleeves reached just below the elbows, and that the hem came within seven and a half inches of the floor.

Not content with example and reproof, legislators in several states introduced bills to reform feminine dress once and for all. The *New York American* reported in 1921 that a bill was pending in Utah providing fine and imprisonment for those who wore on the streets "skirts higher than three inches above the ankle." A bill was laid before the Virginia legislature which would forbid any woman from wearing shirtwaists or evening gowns which displayed "more than three inches of her throat." In Ohio the proposed limit of decolletage was two inches; the bill introduced in the Ohio legislature aimed also to prevent the sale of any "garment which unduly displays or accentuates the lines of the female figure," and to prohibit any "female over fourteen years of age" from wearing "a skirt which does not reach to that part of the foot known as the instep."

Meanwhile innumerable families were torn with dissension over cigarettes and gin and all-night automobile rides. Fathers and mothers lay awake asking themselves whether their children were not utterly lost; sons and daughters evaded questions, lied miserably and unhappily, or flared up to reply rudely that at least they were not dirty-minded hypocrites, that they saw no harm in what they were doing and proposed to go right on doing it. From those liberal clergymen and teachers who prided themselves on keeping step with all that was new, came a chorus of reassurance: these young people were at least franker and more honest than their elders had been; having experimented for themselves, would they not soon find out which standards were outworn and which represented the accumulated moral wisdom of the race? Hearing such hopeful words, many good people took heart again. Perhaps this flare-up of youthful passion was a flash in the pan, after all. Perhaps in another year or two the boys and girls would come to their senses and everything would be all right again.

They were wrong, however. For the revolt of the younger generation was only the beginning of a revolution in manners and morals that was already beginning to affect men and women of every age in every part of the country.

A number of forces were working together and interacting upon one another to make this revolution inevitable.

First of all was the state of mind brought about by the war and its conclusion. A whole generation had been infected by the eat-drink-and-be-merry-for-tomorrow-we-die spirit which accompanied the departure of the soldiers to the training camps and the fighting front. There had been an epidemic not only of abrupt war marriages, but of less conventional liaisons. In France, two million men had found themselves very close to filth and annihilation and very far from the American moral code and its defenders; prostitution had followed the flag and willing mademoiselles from Armentières had been plentiful; American girls sent over as nurses and war workers had come under the influence of continental manners and standards without being subject to the rigid protections thrown about their continental sisters of the respectable classes; and there had been a very widespread and very natural breakdown of traditional restraints, reticences and taboos. It was impossible for this generation to return unchanged when the ordeal was over. Some of them had acquired under the pressure of war-time conditions a new code which seemed to them quite defensible; millions of them had been provided with an emotional stimulant from which it was not easy to taper off. Their torn nerves craved the anodynes of speed, excitement, and passion. They found themselves expected to settle down into the humdrum routine of American life as if nothing had happened, to accept the moral dicta of elders who seemed to them still to be living in a Pollyanna land of rosy ideals which the war had killed for them. They couldn't do it, and they very disrespectfully said so.

"The older generation had certainly pretty well ruined this world before passing it on to us," wrote one of them

(John F. Carter in the *Atlantic Monthly*, September, 1920), expressing accurately the sentiments of innumerable contemporaries. "They give us this thing, knocked to pieces, leaky, red-hot, threatening to blow up; and then they are surprised that we don't accept it with the same attitude of pretty, decorous enthusiasm with which they received it, way back in the 'eighties."

The middle generation was not so immediately affected by the war neurosis. They had had time enough, before 1917, to build up habits of conformity not easily broken down. But they, too, as the letdown of 1919 followed the war, found themselves restless and discontented, in a mood to question everything that had once seemed to them true and worthy and of good report. They too had spent themselves and wanted a good time. They saw their juniors exploring the approaches to the forbidden land of sex, and presently they began to play with the idea of doing a little experimenting of their own. The same disillusion which had defeated Woodrow Wilson and had caused strikes and riots and the Big Red Scare furnished a culture in which the germs of the new freedom could grow and multiply.

The revolution was accelerated also by the growing independence of the American woman. She won the suffrage in 1920. She seemed, it is true, to be very little interested in it once she had it; she voted, but mostly as the unregenerate men about her did, despite the efforts of women's clubs and the League of Women Voters to awaken her to womanhood's civic opportunity; feminine candidates for office were few, and some of them—such as Governor Ma Ferguson of Texas—scarcely seemed to represent the starry-eyed spiritual influence which, it had been promised, would presently ennoble public life. Few of the younger women could rouse themselves to even a passing interest in politics: to them it was a sordid and futile business, without flavor and without hope. Nevertheless, the winning of the suffrage had its effect. It consolidated woman's position as man's equal.

Even more marked was the effect of woman's growing independence of the drudgeries of housekeeping. Smaller houses were being built, and they were easier to look after. Families were moving into apartments, and these made even less claim upon the housekeeper's time and energy. Women were learning how to make lighter work of the preparation of meals. Sales of canned foods were growing, the number of delicatessen stores had increased three times as fast as the population during the decade 1910–20, the output of bakeries increased by 60 per cent during the decade 1914–24. Much of what had once been housework was now either moving out of the home entirely or being simplified by machinery. The use of commercial laundries, for instance, increased by 57 per cent between 1914 and 1924. Electric washing-machines and electric irons were coming to the aid of those who still did their washing at home; the manager of the local electric power company at "Middletown," a typical small American city, estimated in 1924 that nearly 90 per cent of the homes in the city already had electric irons. The housewife was learning to telephone her shopping orders, to get her clothes ready-made and spare herself the rigors of dress-making, to buy a vacuum cleaner and emulate the lovely carefree girls in the magazine advertisements who banished dust with such delicate fingers. Women were slowly becoming emancipated from routine to "live their own lives."

And what were these "own lives" of theirs to be like? Well, for one thing, they could take jobs. Up to this time girls of the middle classes who had wanted to "do something" had been largely restricted to school-teaching, social-service work, nursing, stenography, and clerical work in business houses. But now they poured out of the schools and colleges into all manner of new occupations. They besieged the offices of publishers and advertisers; they went into tea-room management until there threatened to be more purveyors than consumers of chicken patties and cinnamon toast; they sold antiques, sold real estate, opened smart little shops, and finally invaded the department stores. In 1920 the department store was in the mind of the average college girl a rather bourgeois institution which employed "poor shop girls"; by the end of the decade college girls were standing in line for openings in the misses' sports-wear department and even selling behind the counter in the hope that some day fortune might smile upon them and make them buyers or stylists. Small-town girls who once would have been contented to stay in Sauk Center all their days were now borrowing from father to go to New York or Chicago to seek their fortunes—in Best's or Macy's or Marshall Field's. Married women who were encumbered with children and could not seek jobs consoled themselves with the thought that home-making and child-rearing were really "professions," after all. No topic was so furiously discussed at luncheon tables from one end of the country to the other as the question whether the married woman should take a job, and whether the mother had a right to. And as for the unmarried woman, she no longer had to explain why she worked in a shop or an office; it was idleness, nowadays, that had to be defended.

With the job—or at least the sense that

the job was a possibility—came a feeling of comparative economic independence. With the feeling of economic independence came a slackening of husbandly and parental authority. Maiden aunts and unmarried daughters were leaving the shelter of the family roof to install themselves in kitchenette apartments of their own. For city-dwellers the home was steadily becoming less of a shrine, more of a dormitory—a place of casual shelter where one stopped overnight on the way from the restaurant and the movie theater to the office. Yet even the job did not provide the American woman with that complete satisfaction which the management of a mechanized home no longer furnished. She still had energies and emotions to burn; she was ready for the revolution.

Like all revolutions, this one was stimulated by foreign propaganda. It came, however, not from Moscow, but from Vienna. Sigmund Freud had published his first book on psychoanalysis at the end of the nineteenth century, and he and Jung had lectured to American psychologists as early as 1909, but it was not until after the war that the Freudian gospel began to circulate to a marked extent among the American lay public. The one great intellectual force which had not suffered disrepute as a result of the war was science; the more-or-less educated public was now absorbing a quantity of popularized information about biology and anthropology which gave a general impression that men and women were merely animals of a rather intricate variety, and that moral codes had no universal validity and were often based on curious superstitions. A fertile ground was ready for the seeds of Freudianism, and presently one began to hear even from the lips of flappers that "science taught" new and disturbing things about sex. Sex, it appeared, was the central and pervasive force which moved mankind. Almost every human motive was attributable to it: if you were patriotic or liked the violin, you were in the grip of sex—in a sublimated form. The first requirement of mental health was to have an uninhibited sex life. If you would be well and happy, you must obey your libido. Such was the Freudian gospel as it imbedded itself in the American mind after being filtered through the successive minds of interpreters and popularizers and guileless readers and people who had heard guileless readers talk about it. New words and phrases began to be bandied about the cocktail-tray and the Mah Jong table—inferiority complex, sadism, masochism, Œdipus complex. Intellectual ladies went to Europe to be analyzed; analysts plied their new trade in American cities, conscientiously transferring the affections of their fair patients to themselves; and clergymen who preached about the virtue of self-control were reminded by outspoken critics that self-control was out-of-date and really dangerous.

The principal remaining forces which accelerated the revolution in manners and morals were all 100 per cent American. They were prohibition, the automobile, the confession and sex magazines, and the movies.

When the Eighteenth Amendment was ratified, prohibition seemed, . . . to have an almost united country behind it. Evasion of the law began immediately, however, and strenuous and sincere opposition to it—especially in the large cities of the North and East—quickly gathered force. The results were the bootlegger, the speak-easy, and a spirit of deliberate revolt which in many communities made drinking "the thing to do." From these facts in turn flowed further results: the increased popularity of distilled as against fermented liquors, the use of the hip-flask, the cocktail party, and the general transformation of drinking from a masculine prerogative to one shared by both sexes together. The old-time saloon had been overwhelmingly masculine; the speakeasy usually catered to both men and women. As Elmer Davis put it, "The old days when father spent his evenings at Cassidy's bar with the rest of the boys are gone, and probably gone forever; Cassidy may still be in business at the old stand and father may still go down there of evenings, but since prohibition mother goes down with him." Under the new régime not only the drinks were mixed, but the company as well.

Meanwhile a new sort of freedom was being made possible by the enormous increase in the use of the automobile, and particularly of the closed car. (In 1919 hardly more than 10 per cent of the cars produced in the United States were closed; by 1924 the percentage had jumped to 43, by 1927 it had reached 82.8). The automobile offered an almost universally available means of escaping temporarily from the supervision of parents and chaperons, or from the influence of neighborhood opinion. Boys and girls now thought nothing, as the Lynds pointed out in *Middletown,* of jumping into a car and driving off at a moment's notice — without asking anybody's permission — to a dance in another town twenty miles away, where they were strangers and enjoyed a freedom impossible among their neighbors. The closed car, moreover, was in effect a room protected from the weather which could be occupied at any time of the day or night and could be moved at will into a darkened byway or a country lane. The Lynds quoted the judge of the juvenile court in "Middletown" as declaring that the automobile had become a "house of prostitution on wheels," and cited the fact that of thirty girls brought before his court in a year on charges of sex crimes, for whom the place where the offense had occurred was recorded, nineteen were listed as having committed it in an automobile.

Finally, as the revolution began, its influence fertilized a bumper crop of sex magazines, confession magazines, and lurid motion pictures, and these in turn had their effect on a class of readers and movie-goers who had never heard and never would hear of Freud and the libido. The publishers of the sex adventure magazines, offering stories with such titles as "What I Told My Daughter the Night Before Her Marriage," "Indolent Kisses," and "Watch Your Step-Ins," learned to a nicety the gentle art of arousing the reader without arousing the censor. The publishers of the confession magazines, while always instructing their authors to provide a moral ending and to utter pious sentiments, concentrated on the description of what they euphemistically called "missteps." Most of their fiction was faked to order by hack writers who could write one day "The Confessions of a Chorus Girl" and the next day recount, again in the first person, the temptations which made it easy for the taxidriver to go wrong. Both classes of magazines became astonishingly numerous and successful. Bernarr McFadden's *True-Story,* launched as late as 1919, had over 300,000 readers by 1923; 848,000 by 1924; over a million and a half by 1925; and almost two million by 1926 — a record of rapid growth probably unparalleled in magazine publishing.

Crowding the news stands along with the sex and confession magazines were motion-picture magazines which depicted "seven movie kisses" with such captions as "Do you recognize your little friend, Mae Busch? She's had lots of kisses, but she never seems to grow *blasé*. At least you'll agree that she's giving a good imitation of a person enjoying this one." The movies themselves, drawing millions to their doors every day and every night, played incessantly upon the same lucrative theme. The producers of one picture advertised "brilliant men, beautiful jazz babies, champagne baths, midnight revels, petting parties in the purple dawn, all ending in one terrific smashing climax that makes you gasp"; the venders of another promised "neckers, petters, white kisses, red kisses, pleasure-mad daughters, sensation-craving mothers, . . . the truth—bold, naked, sensational." Seldom did the films offer as much as these advertisements promised, but there was enough in some of them to cause a sixteen-year-old girl (quoted by Alice Miller Mitchell) to testify, "Those pictures with hot love-making in them, they make girls and boys sitting together want to get up and walk out, go off somewhere, you know. Once I walked out with a boy before the picture was even over. We took a ride. But my friend, she all the time had to get up and go out with her boy friend."

A storm of criticism from church organizations led the motion-picture producers, early in the decade, to install Will H. Hays, President Harding's Postmaster-General, as their arbiter of morals and of taste, and Mr. Hays promised that all would be well. "This industry must have," said he before the Los Angeles Chamber of Commerce, "toward that sacred thing, the mind of a child, toward that clean virgin thing, that unmarked slate, the same responsibility, the same care about the impressions made upon it, that the best clergyman or the most inspired teacher of youth would have." The result of Mr. Hay's labors in behalf of the unmarked slate was to make the moral ending as obligatory as in the confession magazines, to smear over sexy pictures with pious platitudes, and to blacklist for motion-picture production many a fine novel and play which, because of its very honesty, might be construed as seriously or intelligently questioning the traditional sex ethics of the small town. Mr. Hays, being something of a genius, managed to keep the churchmen at bay. Whenever the threats of censorship began to become ominous he would promulgate a new series of moral commandments for the producers to follow. Yet of the practical effects of his supervision it is perhaps enough to say that the quotations given above all date from the period of his dictatorship. Giving lip-service to the old code, the movies diligently and with consummate vulgarity publicized the new.

Each of these diverse influences—the post-war disillusion, the new status of women, the Freudian gospel, the automobile, prohibition, the sex and confession magazines, and the movies—had its part in bringing about the revolution. Each of them, as an influence, was played upon by all the others; none of them could alone have changed to any great degree the folkways of America; together their force was irresistible.

As Professor of English at the University of Michigan, JOHN W. ALDRIDGE specializes in modern literature and criticism. His book *After the Lost Generation* (1951) includes a penetrating analysis of the young American writers who fled to Paris after World War I. What are these expatriates revolting against? Does their sojourn abroad reflect a philosophical search for new answers or a destructive pessimism? Has the intensity of the expatriate movement been distorted by Aldridge's focus on a select group whose memoirs and accounts of each other may have been exaggerated?*

John W. Aldridge

The Expatriate Rebellion

From this sense of physical isolation and spiritual emptiness, it was easy for the young men to take the next logical step—active, conscious revolt and self-exile from a country which was neither gay enough nor cultured enough to deserve their presence. The idea of exile, like the idea of the religion of art, grew out of their need to sustain the emotions which the war had aroused in them, to keep up the incessant movement, the incessant search for excitement, and to find another faith to replace the one they had lost in the war.

Conveniently, a formal philosophical structure for such ideas had been shaping itself both before and during the war years in the writings of certain prominent social-literary critics, among them H. L. Mencken and Van Wyck Brooks. For a number of years these men had been expressing grave concern for the plight of the sensitive artist in a machine-made, standardized society. It seemed to them that life in America was tawdry, cheap, colorless, and given over to the exclusive worship of wealth and machinery; that for a young writer to do his best work in such a society was impossible. In 1921, Harold Stearns's symposium, *Civilization in the United States*, gave these ideas detailed and scholarly expansion. The thirty intellectuals whom Stearns had gathered together examined in essay form as many phases of American life and came up with the same conclusions: life in America is not worth living. If the young artist is to preserve his talent, he must leave the country. He must, as Stearns urged in his own essay, go to Europe where the creative life is still possible. To show that he meant it, Stearns left for France soon after his book was delivered to the publisher, and, whether because of his example or not, hundreds of the young men followed.

The story of what happened during those years abroad has been written and rewritten many times over. The process of exile was complete. The young men came to Paris. With their wives and children, cats and typewriters, they settled in flats and studios along the Left Bank and in the Latin Quarter. They took jobs as foreign correspondents for American newspapers, sent back social gossip and racing news; wrote book reviews, magazine articles, and stories; bet on horses, gambled, borrowed, and begged; did anything to keep alive and to prolong the show. If we can believe the stories, they were drunk much of the time, traveled considerably, and had a great many love affairs. They also managed to get an impressive amount of good writing done. The early work of Hemingway, Fitzgerald, Dos Passos, Cummings, and others bears witness to the fact. Betweentimes, when they were not drinking at the cafés, partying, or making love, they talked a lot and did a certain amount of thinking. At about this time, some of them discovered Gertrude Stein, and she, in turn, discovered among them talents worthy of her guidance. It was she, perhaps more than any other, who taught them how to make the most of their "lostness," how to develop, as had Sherwood Anderson, an idiom that would be true of their time and truly their own.

Then, as the new writing began to appear, new little magazines began springing up to accommodate it. Their titles, *Broom, transition, This Quarter, Secession,* were indicative of their editorial policies. Fresh currents of energy were breaking out everywhere, everywhere the accent was on the new and different, the departure from old forms and techniques, the rebellion. The years of European apprenticeship were paying off in a vigorous new literature, a literature written so compellingly, with such a tragic sense of loss, that it seemed to describe the predicament of all contemporary humanity. For writers like Hemingway, Dos Passos, and Cummings, the experience of their generation—the bitterness, the monumental disbelief which the war had taught—was the only tradition. They had been uprooted from the world of their childhood with its unwavering ideals and trusts and plunged into the world of Caporetto, the Western front, the "enormous rooms" of the war; and they had awakened from the war only to find themselves in another and even more fantastic world—that of Dada, surrealism, and Gertrude Stein. If they understood only the immediate present and past, if they worshiped only the gods of sex, liquor, violence, and art, it was because they had known nothing else. Life for them would forever after be perceived and lived within the frame of the war and the emotions of war.

Thus, while Mencken and Lewis were still discovering the banalities of life back home, the young men who had acted on their indictments and fled to Europe were discovering a new language which would express themselves and their own unique experience. In Gertrude Stein the demands of a persistent originality had led to greater and greater indulgence in pure technique. Hers was an art deprived of its objective basis, lost somewhere in the convolutions of its careless meaning. The search for every-widening suggestiveness carried the older Joyce into the limbo of dream, the ultimate subjective state beyond the necessity of words. But the young Hemingway's search for the "real thing," "the exact sequence of motion and fact which made the emotion," ended in a prose that was as crystal-clear as brook water, that was written "without tricks and without cheating," with nothing that would "go bad afterwards." Hemingway in those years was the American compromise with Dada. He was everybody's example of an American who combined the best that was in America with the zeal and discipline of the French. He was coarsely, robustly healthy in the tradition of Mark Twain and Sherwood Anderson, but he was never vulgar, almost never naive; and in his passion for exactitude, *le mot juste,* he could only be compared with Flaubert.

This is not to say that Hemingway's was the only or even the most typical new style in the exile literature. E. E. Cummings's nervous, syncopated prose in *The Enormous Room* caught as accurately the sensibility of a world stunned by a prevailing sense of defeat; but his was a less restrained, though equally self-conscious; approach. Cummings had a more acute sense of rebellion than Hemingway. He was breaking the same ground stylistically, but he was doing it with a self-conscious violence and consequently a less steady hand. The result was a prose that struck through the pretensions of the past at the same time that it parodied them, a prose that suited itself instantly to the quick-reflexed life it was describing, and that contained the stomping discords and tingling minor harmonies of an intricate jazz symphony. If it bore little resemblance to Hemingway's prose, its purpose was nonetheless the same: to express the truth of the thing as it was at the

moment it occurred, the truth stripped down to such an ultimate nakedness that, as Hemingway put it, it would be "as valid in a year or ten years or, with luck and if you stated it purely enough, always." Both men succeeded so well in conveying this exact truth, the precise emotions of despair and loss as they had known them, that these emotions were given a special currency and validity and seemed to explain the entire generation to itself and the world. Gertrude Stein had given the key to Hemingway when she had said, "You are all a lost generation," and Hemingway had written a novel around it. Now her words became the slogan of the new literature, and all the young men were trying to live up to them.

One could of course as easily make a god of lostness—and thus be saved—as one could be lost. One could think of it as an intellectual fashion rather than a condition of life and adopt its values in place of having no values at all. Besides, if one believed in nothing one was obliged to practice the rituals of nothingness, and these were good and pleasurable. One could drink and make love all night and still be holy. Yes, and if one carried it far enough, one could even reduce one's art to a deliberate exercise in futility. It was one of the ironies of art, as it was one of the ironies of the doctrine of loss, that beyond a certain point it merged with and became its opposite: the religion of art became irreligion and the lack of values became itself a value.

In the exile colony the process really began with Stein and Joyce when they renounced their native traditions and took on the traditions of pure art. It began, in other words, as it began for Hemingway and Cummings, with a search for absolutes; but it carried beyond them, and in the work of other, less dedicated writers it was turned into a process of general rebellion and misdirected defiance—rebellion against the ends which art was intended to serve and defiance of the public which would not understand those ends. If Stein and Joyce had been victimized by the idiot world and driven into the temple of art, then art would be devoted exclusively to the befuddlement of the world, and the purpose which Stein and Joyce had determined to preserve would be cast down. Art in the hands of the Dadaists was an instrument of confusion; and the obscurity which was once only the accidental by-product of an isolated, religiously fervid talent became in them the sole aim of the artist.

Dada might be said to have contained in the extremest form nearly all the attitudes on which the exile literary movement was based. If, as Malcolm Cowley has suggested, the reader of Joyce was expected to master a dozen languages, be familiar with the mythology of all races, and memorize the map of Dublin, in order to comprehend him, if the reader of Stein was helpless without her personal key to understanding, the reader of a Dada poem or novel could not hope, either through learning or a lifelong acquaintanceship with the author, to unravel a meaning. Dada, according to its adherents, had no meaning. It was dedicated to "pure" and "absolute" art. "Art," the Dada Manifesto read, "is a private matter; the artist does it for himself; any work of art that can be understood is the product of a journalist."

Dada was thus the extreme of individualism. It coupled an open rejection of audience with the belief that all communication between men was impossible. But perhaps in no other respect was Dada more typical of the tendencies of exile than in its active defiance of the world.

Defiance, contemptuous rebellion, had been the motive power behind the entire expatriate movement as it had been the first principle of the religion of art. A generation of priests had defied the old commandments: a generation of Stephen Dedaluses had borne their chalices "safely through a throng of foes." But where the defiance of the chosen had led to flight, the defiance of Dada led to open war. The world, said Dada, "left in the hands of bandits, is in a state of madness, aggressive and complete madness.". . . "Let each man cry: there is a great labor of destruction and negation to perform. We must sweep and clean.". . . "What there is within us of the divine is the awakening of anti-human action." The duty of the artist was clear: he must expend upon the world the full measure of his contempt, and he must "protest with all the fists of his being" all assertions of humanity and life. And what of his duty to his art? Art was the weapon of his disgust. Its needs were always subordinate to the destructive function it was set to perform. Art, therefore, was anti-art, dedicated to its own eventual suicide.

Armed with such a view Dada marched upon the helpless world. To the accompaniment of ringing electric bells and deafening shouts and laughter from the audience, meetings were held, poems and articles were read that no one could hear, drawings done in chalk were exhibited and erased on the stage. At one meeting Tristan Tzara, the founder of Dada, recalls "thousands of people of all classes manifested very uproariously it is impossible to say exactly what—their joy or their disapproval, by unexpected cries and general laughter, which constituted a very pretty accompaniment to the manifestoes read by six people at once. The newspapers said that an old man in the audience gave himself up to behavior of a character more or less intimate, that somebody set off some flash-light powder and that a pregnant woman had to be taken out." At another "twelve hundred people were turned away. There were three spectators for every seat; it was suffocating. Enthusiastic members of the audience had brought musical instruments to interrupt us. . . . I invented . . . a diabolical machine composed of a klaxon and three successive invisible echoes, for the purpose of impressing on the minds of the audience certain phrases describing the aims of Dada. . . . It was impossible to hear a single word. . . ." There were always meetings, demonstrations (sometimes in churches, once in a public urinal), "manifestations" of Dada policy. There were even Dada trials and theatrical performances that ended usually with fights on the stage and the intervention of the police. But even at the height of its bustling activity, there was something ineffectual about Dada. Its protests were directed against no specific injustice, toward no social reform. The freedom it fought for and finally won was used to no purpose. The most exciting of its gestures were merely phantom poundings on a wall that offered no resistance.

Yet beneath its monstrous wastefulness and hollow disdain, Dada was alive. If its achievements as a doctrine, as an extreme of art, were poor and few, its influence as a stimulus to action for others, for the entire age, was great. The phenomenon of Dada cannot, in fact, be separated from the whole restless spirit of the Twenties; for in it all the roads of exile converged and the best and worst possibilities of the exile ideal were realized. From Dada, it was only a short step to the "nada hail nada full of nada" of Hemingway, the sociological zero of Dos Passos, the romantic hopelessness of Fitzgerald, the "nothing again nothing" of

Eliot, the "indefinite refusal to be anything whatsoever" of Valéry, the implicit denial of society in Stein and Joyce—even to the "lost, ah lost" of Wolfe. Dada was everywhere; its ghost in a hundred manifestations haunted the literature of a decade. If Dada had no meaning, it had an infinite capacity to suggest meaning. "If you must speak of Dada you must speak of Dada. If you must not speak of Dada you must still speak of Dada."

And I believe the final effect of Dada as well as of the religion of art and the doctrine of negation was a salutary one. The creative energy which was short-circuited in Dada found release elsewhere and spread through the writing of the Twenties like a prairie fire; protest and denial gave that writing a single point of view, a unified plan of attack, and the impetus of rebellion carried it away from the narrow traditions of the past and toward new and startling discoveries in form and technique. The indignation and sense of having been betrayed which the Lost Generation brought out of the war was expressed in a fearless realism that exploited until then forbidden subject matter; while the teachings of the religion of art, self-consuming though they were when fanatically carried out, gave those writers an awareness of artistic mission, a feeling of belonging to a special priesthood with special requirements which they were bound by holy order to live up to. If despair and disillusion were negative values, they were at least good values for the literature of the time, and they were better than no values at all.

But Dada was destined to die as the exile was destined to end. In the fall of 1929 when the machinery of art had been grinding away at full speed for nearly a decade, turning out new morals and literary mannerisms so bright and daring that they seemed to presage a magnificent long life for American art abroad, something in the mechanism snapped and the machine began running down. Back home in Wall Street, among the debris of ticker tape and ruined fortunes, lay the remnants of a broken promise, the promise everybody had made to everybody else—that the show would go on forever.

NORMAN F. FURNISS (1922–1964) taught American
intellectual history at Colorado State University in
Fort Collins. He was particularly interested in religious
conflict in the United States, and his major works
include *The Fundamentalist Controversy, 1918–1931*
(1954) and *The Mormon Conflict, 1850–1859* (1960).
Furniss feels the Fundamentalists became more
militant in the 1920s, as nineteenth-century folk
attitudes grew increasingly out of touch with advances
made in science and theology. Why did modernism and
evolution pose such a threat to religious conservatives?
To what extent was the Fundamentalist controversy
an urban-rural conflict?*

Norman F. Furniss

The Fundamentalist Crusade

In 1918 most of the prominent ministers in the United States would have endorsed the opinion that "the warfare of science with theology" was at an end. Certainly the country's scientists anticipated no interference with their work from an angry populace worried over challenges to its faith. But within seven years the wave of fundamentalism had achieved such magnitude that several men feared for the preservation of intellectual freedom. Maynard Shipley, a lecturer on physics and astronomy, formed a society in 1925 to combat the Fundamentalists and wrote magazine articles, pamphlets, and a book in order to awaken the American people to the attack upon scientific investigation. Carl Van Doren, sharing Shipley's concern, envisaged a 1970 America in which there was only one "last heretic," an exponent of evolution and modernism who had unaccountably escaped the "Preliminary Census" of 1929 and even the "Final Inquisition" of 1940.[1] Others reached the conclusion that fundamentalist clergymen controlled from one-fourth to three-fourths of American churches, their power varying in different regions of the country, with a total following of some 20,000,000. Serious observers had reason to be anxious: the movement,

[1] *Century, 107* (1924), 929 ff.

*From Norman F. Furniss, *The Fundamentalist Controversy, 1918–1931* (New Haven: Yale University Press), pp. 14–34. Copyright © 1954 by Yale University Press. Some footnotes omitted by permission.

although not so formidable as these statements suggested, did achieve great proportions in the 1920's.

The principal cause for the rise of the fundamentalist controversy was the incompatibility of the nineteenth-century orthodoxy cherished by many humble Americans with the progress made in science and theology since the Civil War. It is true that in 1918 the important leaders of American protestantism had either accepted the new theories or else turned to aspects of church work other then heresy trials as more productive fields for their labors, but in doing so they had often progressed in their thinking far beyond their own congregations. Many of the people in the pews had been at best only dimly aware that a dispute over theology had ever taken place, and they were no party to any attempt at reconciling science and theology through concession and the reinterpretation of creeds. When, in the years after the World War they came to realize that the doctrines they had accepted as eternal truths were in fact no longer held by their pastors, they energetically set about defending their beliefs. The belated assertion of inherited views, clashing with seemingly antithetical affirmations, thus lay at the base of the fundamentalist controversy.

The conservatives awoke to see their authoritative faith attacked from two directions. In the first place modernism, that movement stemming from higher criticism which had discarded outgrown views of the Scriptures, struck at the heart of the orthodox creed. To the Fundamentalists, religious beliefs formed a pyramid, each tenet resting on the one below, with the infallible Bible as the broad foundation; to reshape one block, to remove another, would send the whole structure crashing to the ground. Throughout the vicissitudes of theological interpretation and compromise, the force of custom had preserved such reasoning intact within a large stratum of society, ready for use when a Bryan or a Riley issued the call. In *Elmer Gantry* Sinclair Lewis had one of his characters say of the tendency to cling to inherited beliefs: "All you have to do with [Baptists or Methodists] is to get some perfectly meaningless doctrine and keep repeating it. You won't bore the layman-in fact the only thing that they resent is something new, so they won't have to use their brains."[2] In a more charitable manner John M. Mecklin, Dartmouth sociologist, wrote of a typical Mississippi Fundamentalist: "The theological formulas and ritualistic symbols of piety . . . were just as much a part of the texture of his daily life as the impossible animals or flowers of the oriental rug in his parlor. To alter or eliminate these doctrines would have been just as disastrous to the pattern of his daily life as the tearing out of the figures would be to the texture of the rug."[3] Static habits of thought, preventing many people from speculating upon their faith, provided a vast, sympathetic constituency for the fundamentalist agitator.

The theory of evolution presented an even more direct challenge than did modernism. The Bible affirmed that man was the product of fiat creation, molded from the dust of the earth by God's hands, not the chance result of a development untold ages in length. In another way evolution contradicted the Fundamentalists' creed, by indirectly questioning the divinity of Christ. In Darwin's

---

[2] *Elmer Gantry* (New York, Harcourt, Brace, 1927), p. 87.
[3] *My Quest for Freedom* (New York, 1945), p. 251.

hypothesis there seemed to be no room for a supernatural being, no toleration of stories concerning biological miracles.

The writings of the Fundamentalists after 1918 clearly revealed the collision between differing beliefs that was to produce serious controversy. In opposing the suggestions of modernism the orthodox leaders attacked every individual who in any way imputed errors to the biblical narratives, and they defended in an especially belligerent manner the five tenets they considered most essential. Curtis Lee Laws, portly editor of the *Watchman-Examiner,* that moderate but determined voice of conservative Baptists, uncompromisingly rejected any effort at questioning the truth of Christ's resurrection: "It is like saying that the title to the house which you prepared as a habitation for your old age is a fraud . . . It is like saying that the bank in which you have put all the money you have in the world is insolvent. . . . If Jesus Christ did not rise from the dead, we cannot depend upon a word of what he said." Another Fundamentalist who agreed with Laws on the importance of familiar doctrines wrote: "how blessed that some things, after all, are static— the love of God, the way of life, and the revealing Book, that have not changed through all the centuries." . . .

Another cause of the controversy, and one closely akin to the antithesis between orthodox and liberal beliefs, lay in the conservatives' firm conviction that modernism and evolution, in questioning their cherished doctrines, would destroy Christianity as a moral force in the nation. Numerous factors—the unhappy effects of the war, the rising industrialization of the country, increased opportunity for secular activity on Sunday— had indeed hindered the march of faith in the United States after 1918. The Fundamentalists seized upon the postwar apathy toward institutionalized protestantism to show that the new currents of thought would, if unchecked, soon create a "pagan America." To them the coincidence between an apparent loss of religious conviction in the country and a popular acceptance of unsubstantiated theories was proof in itself that only atheism could result from abandoning orthodox Christianity.

One detailed analysis of declining interest in the church made a profound impression upon the Fundamentalists, who received it as verification of the insidious work of modernism and evolution. In 1916 James Henry Leuba, a professor of psychology at Bryn Mawr, published *The Belief in God and Immortality,* a study of college students which showed that these young people had suffered a decided loss of faith during their four years' exposure to modern ideas. While Percy Stickney Grant, an Episcopalian clergyman, saw the answer to the problem in the necessity for improving methods of religious instruction, the conservatives considered the book documented evidence of the bankruptcy of science and liberal theology. Bryan's friends maintained that Leuba's survey was the chief cause for the Commoner's entrance into the controversy, an accurate conclusion if one may judge by the many angry references to Leuba's book in Bryan's speeches and articles. The work became so valuable a weapon to Fundamentalists that they used it as late as 1935, nineteen years after its publication, to justify their efforts and to condemn their opponents. Several essays dealing with the faith of American soldiers, appearing shortly after the cessation of hostilities, seemed to supplement Leuba's conclusion on the growing skepticism among the nation's youth and further strengthened suspicions concerning the dire effects of modernism and evolution.

The conviction that the theories of the day were responsible for manifest evils gained strength from the wave of anti-communist hysteria which swept the country immediately after the war. In their writings and speeches Riley, Price, and Bryan frequently used this fear to enlist supporters for their various campaigns. Communism, they pointed out, deliberately rejected God, ridiculed the Scriptures, and glorified power. Was not modernism, they asked, an attempt to reduce the Deity to an intangible cosmic force and to cast doubt upon the infallible Bible? What was evolution other than a philosophical glorification of brutality, of the struggle of beasts for survival? . . .

Excessively radical and careless statements by several writers strengthened the conservatives in their conclusion that novel ideas in science and theology were responsible for agnosticism, atheism, and communism. James B. Bury added fuel to the fire by his comment: "If intelligence has anything to do with this bungling process [evolution], it would be an intelligence infinitely low. And the finished product, if regarded as a work of design, points to incompetence in the designer."[4] Price indignantly warned his readers that Huxley, in *The Destiny of Man*, had this to say about the efficacy of Christian ethics: "'For his successful progress from the savage state man has been largely indebted to those qualities which he shared with the ape and the tiger.'"[5] But it was not always the mature scholar who evoked anger by startling observation. In the period after the World War young teachers who had not fully understood or assimilated what they had heard in college often delighted in shocking their audiences by dwelling upon the advances in scientific discovery and the significance of such accomplishments. When scientists probed too far, the *Methodist Review* accurately warned, or when they casually attempted to discuss causes in non-religious or irreligious terms, they invited the Fundamentalists to spring to the defense of their beliefs.

Liberal preachers were equally guilty of fanning the conservatives' wrath by incautious remarks. The *Presbyterian of the South* observed that the "Rev. William Norman Guthrie, rector of St. Mark's in the Bouwerie, New York, is reported to have said, 'The New Testament is a book written by a lot of chumps, who were thick in the head.'"[6] The learned Episcopalian priest was undoubtedly misquoted (a favorite technique of the Fundamentalists), and yet his rash comments upon the fallibility of the Bible had invited such distortions and thus helped to discredit the work of higher critics. The controversy would have come even if scientists and theologians, whether seasoned or inexperienced, had tempered their public utterances; but their radical statements upon matters vital to the religion of many Americans strengthened the conviction that the new ideas must be crushed before they had made the United States a nation of atheists.

Complete misunderstanding on the part of innumerable fundamentalist leaders concerning the findings of evolution and modernism also contributed to the appearance of the controversy. Had Riley, Bryan, and other

---

[4] *A History of Freedom of Thought* (New York, Henry Holt, 1913), pp. 181–182.

[5] *Back to the Bible*, p. 100.

[6] *Presbyterian of the South, 101* (1927), 1.

influential men chosen to reconcile themselves to the advances made in science and theology, as liberal clergymen had done, there would naturally have been no crusade. But this they were completely unable to do, not only because their inflexible faith appeared utterly opposed to compromise but also because their distorted opinions of evolution and biblical criticism made any reconciliation prohibitively distasteful. Based upon prejudice and ignorance, their misconceptions were of such strength as to produce extreme intolerance and the desire to repress ideas contrary to their beliefs.

To the Fundamentalists, few of whom had read widely in the scholarly treatises of the day, evolution stated that man had descended directly from the ape. Despite the efforts of biologists to explain their views concerning the origin of man, conservative leaders continued to tell their audiences that evolutionists were trying to link them all directly to this humble animal. The monkey became a symbol of derision and a technique of refutation. When attempting to disprove evolution, a Norfolk preacher brought a live monkey to the pulpit and challenged anyone "to stand up and acknowledge common ancestry."[7] In a debate with a professor at the University of West Virginia, Bryan advanced as his most telling argument the question, "From what ape did you descend?"[8] William E. Biederwolf, a widely traveled evangelist, warned his readers that the purpose of evolution was to make mankind the close relation of this unspeakably filthy creature. . . .

In their opposition to evolution the Fundamentalists drew strength from the scientists themselves. When careful investigators took pains to show that they considered few of their propositions eternally true, the orthodox leaders cited their determination to eschew dogmatism as evidence of a lack of confidence in Darwinism. To their evident pleasure the Fundamentalists also found other scholars who were willing to join them in actively disproving and condemning the thesis that man had reached his present state through a long process of development. To the champions of orthodoxy, with their cloudy comprehension of evolutionary theories, the issue could therefore be simply stated: evolution produced disbelief by challenging the truth of the Scriptures, the cornerstone of Christianity, but was itself little more than the product of the wild imaginings of a few men. Bryan, as usual, summed up the stand of the Fundamentalists here: "Why should the Bible, which the centuries have been unable to shake, be discarded for scientific works that have to be revised and corrected every few years?"[9] . . .

Nowhere is the misunderstanding of modernism more clearly displayed than in the disagreement over the figure of Jesus. To conservatives who believed in the literal, infallible Bible, the account of Jesus' birth, life, and death was either true or not true; either God had appeared among men for the purpose of saving them or the narrative was a cruel hoax. With such convictions based upon the word of the Bible, the Fundamentalists could not comprehend the attitude of scholars who thought of the Scriptures as human documents, as the progressive, sometimes cloudy, revelation of God to man. Instead they were persuaded that

---

[7] *News and Observer* (Raleigh), Feb. 17, 1925.
[8] *NYT,* June 5, 1922.

[9] *In His Image,* p. 94.

higher criticism would destroy Christianity entirely by degrading its central figure. One Southern Methodist, after hesitating to pose the question, finally asked ministers who rejected the doctrine of the Virgin Birth: "Have you considered the taint and the stain you place upon Jesus and upon Mary, his mother?"[10] Another was more outspoken: "The Modernist juggles the Scripture statements of His deity and denies His virgin birth, making Him a Jewish bastard, born out of wedlock, and stained forever with the shame of His mother's immorality."[11] As the author of the Tennessee anti-evolution law believed, evolution and modernism made Jesus a charlatan.

The Fundamentalists opposed the challenges to their theology in two ways. On the one hand, they advanced evidence supporting the truth of the biblical narratives said to be mythical by the Modernists. Assuming that, if any errors in the assertions of higher criticism could be found, the entire method must be scrapped, W. B. Riley used recent archaeological discoveries to defend the validity of many statements of fact in the Old Testament once challenged as inaccurate. Riley's researches strengthened his conclusion that "for full fifty years every turn of the archaeological spade had proven the moral dishonesty and scientific inaccuracy of Bible opponents."[12] Harry Rimmer was later to undertake a more detailed defense of scriptural truthfulness running to six volumes in the so-called John Lawrence Frost Memorial Library. But most Fundamentalists were unprepared for a schol-

arly justification of their beliefs and so turned to the second means of crushing heresy, an aggressive attempt to stamp out the views of their theological opponents and to force orthodoxy upon all.

The World War's great impact upon the nation strengthened in several ways the determination of conservatives to combat the new forms of knowledge. In the first place, the catastrophe caused many to reject the optimism once inspired by the theory of evolution, the concept of man's inevitable, continuous advance to a state of universal felicity, and instead focused their hope upon one of the five major points of the fundamentalist creed, the Second Coming. Again the propaganda of hatred, so useful in arousing passions against America's wartime enemies, produced during the subsequent years of peace an unanticipated harvest of bitterness and insecurity that lingered in the spirits of many orthodox people, preparing them for an ideological crusade upon unacceptable beliefs at home. And finally the Fundamentalists made use of the Allies' condemnation of the materialistic philosophy of Germany to brand modernism as an alien, perverting faith, since it was the product of an aspect of that philosophy.

The theory of evolution had provided men with a cheerful outlook as they entered the twentieth century, for it fostered the conviction that nothing could prevent the human race from creating, slowly or rapidly, a good society free of evils. The terrible sight of a world at war, arising so unexpectedly before the eyes of Americans, destroyed such expectations and led many, especially those who had never been satisfied with the assumptions of evolution, to subject the religious liberals' affirmations to hostile analysis. They decided that modernism, with its synthesis of Christianity and evolution, had

---

[10] *Christian Advocate, 82* (1921), 936–937.

[11] J. E. Conant, *The Church, the Schools, and Evolution* (Chicago, Bible Institute Colportage Association, 1922), pp. 32–33.

[12] *Inspiration or Evolution*, p. 17.

displayed its complete fallaciousness, since it had been unable to prevent the holocaust despite its high-sounding aspirations for man's progress. Whereas numerous liberal churchmen took the lesson to be opposition to war in any form, the Fundamentalists demanded that the whole discredited theology be scrapped in favor of a return to the traditional beliefs of Christianity, valid for all time. In the words of a character in one of his books George McCready Price summed up the conservatives' attitude: "'But Colonel,' broke in the Pastor fervently, 'it is not merely that the evolutionists and the Socialists have a different account of the origin of the human race than is found in the Bible, but their substitution is entirely inadequate to meet the world's needs.'"[13]

In reaction to the Modernists' optimism the Fundamentalists, convinced that the war presaged the end of the world, placed their hope upon the Second Coming of Christ. This tenet explained the evil days to their satisfaction, for it envisaged, so far as most Adventists were concerned, a period of devastation before the Return. But since the doctrine of Christ's reappearance on earth was one of the beliefs which the Fundamentalists felt to be jeopardized by the higher critics' tinkering with the Bible, the emphasis on millennialism demanded of them a spirited defense of the old faith and bitter opposition to the new. It was significant that many fervent champions of religious orthodoxy after 1918 were premillennialists. . . .

In the 1920's the figure of the deceitful Modernist was as familiar to the conservatives as the gaunt, sharp-nosed Puritan to the anti-prohibition forces. The *King's*

Business, a publication of the Bible Institute of Los Angeles, observed of the "creeping critics": "These men do not knock at the door, make themselves known and reveal their purpose, but have *secretly slipped* in *sideways;* and once safely inside, they have secretly, shrewdly and satanically laid their plans to foist upon the saints their doctrine of denial of God's holy word."[14] A parable jumped to Riley's mind in this connection: "The tares of Evolution have been surreptitiously sown. It was night, and under cover of darkness the enemy came, not in the early evening when people were moving about, lest he be detected, but later, when men slept and no courage was required to put over the dastardly deed."[15] As during the war patriotic Americans felt the enemy secretly sapping the ramparts of the nation, so in the 1920's Fundamentalists continued to see those other agents of Satan, evolution and modernism, clandestinely trying to subvert all that was good.

In yet another way the World War played a part in the outbreak of militant fundamentalism after 1918. During the conflagration Americans had learned through atrocity stories and vague rumors of espionage to hate Germany as a barbaric nation. But to the Fundamentalists higher criticism was a product of the German materialistic philosophy. That nation, they further believed, had followed evolution's theory of the survival of the fittest to its logical conclusion in a ruthless attempt to conquer Europe. They concluded, accordingly, that modernism, combining higher criticism and evolution into an unholy caricature of religion, was only an expression on this

[13] G. M. Price and R. B. Thurber, *Socialism in the Test-tube* (Nashville, Southern Publishing Company, 1921), p. 68.

[14] *The King's Business, 15* (1924), 268.
[15] *Inspiration or Evolution,* p. 124.

continent of a philosophy which had produced the most destructive war of all time, and they carried over into their postwar attacks upon modernism both the hatred and the propagandistic labels used during the years of actual armed conflict. When condemning the theory of evolution they made repeated references to the notion that Nietzsche and his disciples had merely put the hypothesis into practice. Modernism, they further asserted, had transformed Germany into a godless nation capable of any evil deed and would, if permitted, ruin the United States as well.

Whereas the World War played a demonstrable role in the growth of the fundamentalist movement, economic causes of the phenomenon are much less clearly seen. Several competent writers have stated, but without adequate documentation, that economic forces influenced the Fundamentalists in two ways. On the one hand, some believed that large industrialists used the movement to block the Social Gospelers' close investigation of business methods; others maintained that the controversy was at bottom a protest of the rural-agrarian class against urban society. Since the writings of the orthodox leaders reveal but slight support for such interpretations, this study can only present the two explanations for the spread of fundamentalism, together with reference to a few passages from fundamentalist works that would seem to substantiate them. Let us hope that eventually more light may be shed on the question.

The learned Harvard theologian, Kirsopp Lake, best summarized the thesis that found industrialists supporting conservatives for selfish reasons. Lake conjectured: "There is also a more sinister cause which may enormously help Fundamentalism. It may appear to large financial interests that industrial stability can be safeguarded by Fundamentalists who can be trusted to teach 'anti-revolutionary' doctrines in politics and economics as well as in theology."[16] Three other writers have agreed with Lake's analysis, only altering it to make the theory an affirmation. They stated definitely that much of the financial backing of the Fundamentalists came from a number of extremely wealthy men. . . .

A good exposition of the second economic interpretation, which saw in fundamentalism a rural-urban controversy, is that of H. Richard Niebuhr: "Its [fundamentalism's] popular leader was the agrarian W. J. Bryan; its rise coincided with the depression of agricultural values after the World War; it achieved little strength in the urban and industrial sections of the country but was active in many rural states. The opposing religious movement, modernism, was identified on the other hand with bourgeois culture, having its strength in the cities and in the churches supported by the urban middle classes."[17] Several facts seem to support Niebuhr's analysis of the phenomenon. The most rabid anti-evolution agitation was to be found in the primarily rural South, where the farm people played a prominent part in the demand for repressive legislation. Furthermore, the writings of the Fundamentalists at times revealed a definite animus toward the city. A. V. Babbs, in one of his little case studies of redemption, said of a Pinkerton: "Just what the nature of his detective duties had been, none of course knew, but the evil mark of the city was

---

[16] *The Religion of Yesterday and To-morrow* (London, Christophers, 1925), p. 161.

[17] H. Richard Niebuhr, "Fundamentalism," *Encyclopedia of Social Sciences*, eds. E. R. A. Seligman and Alvin Johnson (New York, 1937), *3*, 527.

upon him, and he had certainly met life under conditions which had filled the minds of his friends with alarm, if not with despair."[18] Price had an opinion on urban life, with its movies, tangos, and Wall Streets: "The lesson is for the individual, the family, who wishes to break away from the evil environment of modern Babylon. Out of the cities, back to the land, back to the free air of heaven . . . where all can come face to face with nature and the God of nature."[19]

Although such statements appear to substantiate the belief that the controversy was an expression of a clash between rural and urban America, the conclusion may be challenged. It is true that anti-evolution laws were often introduced by legislators representing the folk in the hills of Tennessee and on the farms of Mississippi; but in those areas it was apparently ignorance of the meaning of modernism and evolution, ignorance then blanketing much of rural America, that brought about the attack, not antagonism toward the cities. The fundamentalist movement arose among people in America who had failed to keep pace with the intellectual progress of the nation after 1870; were not the rural classes for the most part untouched by the developments in science and theology? Their strong reaction against the manifestations of intellectual progress apparently did not arise from an economic collision with urban areas but rather from their sudden awareness after 1918 that their most cherished beliefs differed greatly from those of the city dwellers.

In addition, conservative spokesmen were no more identified with one economic class than they were with one geographical area. Although Bryan was often throughout his life, as in this religious question, the voice of agrarian interests, many important Fundamentalists drew their support from large congregations in such cities as Fort Worth, Minneapolis, and New York. Finally, a survey of the Fundamentalists' writings does not reveal many statements similar to those of Babbs and Price. Since they did not hesitate to express their opinions and predilections on any subject drawing their attention, their books, pamphlets, and articles running to countless millions of words, one must conclude from their lack of reference to a rural-urban disparateness that they were not motivated by the issue. The economic interpretation advanced by Niebuhr is attractive, for it simplifies the study of the controversy, but further evidence is required before it can be accepted.

There is another theory as to the origin of the fundamentalist controversy which, like the economic interpretations, is hard if not impossible to document and so deserves only brief mention. Exponents of this theory maintained that many unscrupulous preachers, conscious of a decline in church attendance after the war and of their own concomitant loss of importance, threw their energies into the crusade against modernism and evolution as a means of building up their congregations. It is true that one characteristic of protestantism in the early 1920's was the widespread use of melodramatic advertising and sermons to attract as many as possible to church. One retired clergyman mentioned with sorrow the sermon subjects that he had seen: "Back Home and Dead Broke" (the prodigal son); "They Satisfy" (the comfort of divine grace); "Eventually, Why Not Now?" (conversion); "Three in One Oil" (the Trinity). It is similarly true that the fundamentalist movement num-

---

[18] Babbs, *Modernistic Poison,* p. 43.
[19] *Back to the Bible,* pp. 219–221.

bered among its leaders men who used every device in their power to attract followers. Some, like J. Frank Norris of Fort Worth and John Roach Straton of New York, revealed an awareness that sensational use of conservative themes resulted in members for their churches and subscribers for their magazines. One figure, Edgar Young Clarke, even tried to find in fundamentalism a way to financial betterment. Yet without further proof it is impossible to ascertain whether many orthodox spokesmen used the crusade to restore their own prestige, then threatened by apathy toward religion, and thus helped to precipitate the whole controversy, or whether, sincerely deploring the new beliefs, they found justification for flamboyant action in the goal they sought.

Such, then, were the major impulses behind the occurrence of militant fundamentalism after 1918—the basic antagonism between the old faith and the new knowledge, the conviction that modernism and evolution were productive of social evils, the impact of the war, and the rest. They were the great catalyzing agents; there were, however, other forces of importance that should be noted.

Bryan's championship of the Fundamentalists' position became in itself an occasion for the rise of the controversy. Until he entered the conflict in 1920 it was of minor significance, despite the conventions and polemics of conservative leaders. Bryan brought to it not only his large personal following, the residue of his political peregrinations, but also his magic voice and moving rhetoric. Capable of turning a phrase as easily as he shed his alpaca coat, Bryan let flow a stream of quotable sentences that could sustain the faith of conservatives and rally them to

a crusade: "If a man believes that he is a descendant of the ape he can go to a zoölogical garden and speculate on how far he has come. If he believes the Bible he goes to church and considers how far he has to go."[20] "I have just as much right as the atheist to begin with an assumption, and I would rather begin with God and reason down, than begin with a piece of dirt and reason up."[21] "I have no use for any man who prefers the blood of the beast to the Blood of the Lamb."[22] As Bryan thundered his denunciations of evolution to the state legislatures, as he aroused the orthodoxy of his audiences with poetic if inaccurate apothegms, the fundamentalist crusade grew to great proportions; after his death it entered a period of rapid decline. Without his support the other champions of the movement—Riley, Norris, Straton—would have been unable to give the dispute national importance.

Another source of the Fundamentalists' strength lay in the amazing energy of their leaders. Visualizing the dispute as a fight to the finish for the preservation of Christianity, they stumped the country, speaking everywhere from pulpit and platform. They never ceased to write, their words flowing forth in books, magazine articles, pamphlets, and in every other form of literature possible. They created organizations to combat evolution and modernism, seminaries to propagate orthodox beliefs, and Bible schools to strengthen the faith of the young. Their names appeared in innumerable lists of directories, trustees, and contributing editors. Years before the liberals had come to realize that the controversy was more than an evanescent tempest, these

---

[20] *NYT,* June 14, 1922.
[21] *In His Image,* p. 14.
[22] *Christian Work, 114* (1923), 650.

men were writing, talking, and working with phrenetic enthusiasm. . . .

If the energy of the fundamentalist leaders was a source of strength for the movement, lack of opposition to their campaigns was another. While in the years before and shortly after the World War Riley and his fellows were forming their battalions, Modernists and evolutionists alike generally ignored the signs of discontent with their affirmations. When after 1922 fundamentalism came into full flower, the liberals were prone to assume an attitude of disdainful sniffing or professed to believe that the plant would soon wither and die. Although eventually many learned societies passed resolutions critical of the Fundamentalists' maneuverings and occasionally went so far as to discuss means of expressing their resistance, only Maynard Shipley's Science League of America fought the anti-evolution bills. In the denominations the liberals formed few societies like the Modern Churchmen's Union of the Episcopalians to preserve their beliefs against men who sought to compel acceptance of orthodox tenets.

Several writers, in discussing this lack of opposition, have found that, especially in the South, fear of a reaction from the people accounted for the failure of the leaders in education to fight for academic freedom. Concern lest angry conservatives cut off public funds from colleges and universities or curtail their enrollments by a boycott persuaded many cautious officials that prudent silence was a better virtue than sturdy defense. In Kentucky and North Carolina, where college presidents Frank L. McVey, William L. Poteat, and Harry W. Chase jeopardized the financial status of their institutions by ardent, public denunciation of anti-evolution proposals, the legislative aspirations of the Fundamentalists did not acquire extensive popular support. On the other hand, wherever the logical leaders of freedom in teaching withheld their opinions, the Fundamentalists enjoyed marked success or at least came close to pushing repressive measures through the legislatures. In Tennessee there was no public figure who dared risk the future of his college by condemning Butler's resolution against the teaching of evolution.

College officials were not alone in their hesitation to challenge the Fundamentalists for fear of retaliation. Editors of southern newspapers, aware that a liberal stand might affect circulation, often were reluctant to reflect any disapprobation of the Fundamentalists' activities, a policy which lasted in Tennessee long after the controversy had abated. When in 1931 the *Literary Digest* requested the important papers of that state to comment on the legislature's refusal to repeal the anti-evolution law, the *Chattanooga Daily Times* alone replied with a strongly worded editorial criticizing the decision. Of the rest, only the *Knoxville Journal* answered in any form, saying in a private letter to the *Digest* that it did not care to comment on the vote and believed that the question should not be raised. So far as the churchmen of the South were concerned, the *Christian Century* found the timidity of Modernists to have played a large part in the Fundamentalists' successes. The publication estimated that, of fifty liberal ministers in Tennessee, perhaps ten had the courage to reveal their theological opinions openly, the others remaining silent either through fear of losing their pulpits or through a desire not to shake the faith of their congregations.

Another element in the lack of opposition to the Fundamentalists was the failure of many people to realize at first the

seriousness of the controversy. To evolutionists and Modernists the issues had
been debated and settled before the turn
of the century; it was difficult for them
to believe that the dispute would start
again. For several years they thought it
enough to reassure the Fundamentalists
that there was no need for conflict. The
American Institute of Sacred Literature
published pleasant little tracts by famous
men on the compatibility of the old faith
and the new knowledge, basing its action
on the misconception that a few soothing
words would be sufficient to restore peace.
In 1923 a group of scientists, among them
Robert Millikan, Michael Pupin, Henry
Fairfield Osborn, and Edwin G. Conklin,
felt that a comfortingly worded "Joint
Statement upon the Relation of Science
and Religion" would dispel the clouds of
doubt in orthodox minds. In conjunction
with other factors, a lack of opposition,
whether from a misunderstanding of the
situation or from economic considerations, accounted for the strength and
success of the Fundamentalists.

A final cause of the controversy resulted
from conditions found in the South alone.
One of the reasons for the strength of the
fundamentalist movement there was that
through it the people expressed their reaction to northern ridicule. The scorn of
Mencken and other caustic writers at
southern backwardness in theological
and scientific thinking aroused in the
people of Tennessee, Mississippi, and
elsewhere an opposition to modernism
and evolution which would have been
less vituperative had the criticism been
more moderate. The northern contention
that the intolerance of "Main Street"
could be found in any town below the
Mason-Dixon line goaded the Fundamentalists there into hostility. Representatives of such northern organizations as

the American Civil Liberties Union and
the American Association for the Advancement of Atheism, as well as many
supercilious reporters who flooded Day-
ton during the Scopes trial, made compromise and understanding impossible by
their laughter and derision.

Sensitivity to northern disparagement
often appeared in the words of southern
Fundamentalists. When a cautious representative warned the legislature of Mississippi that an anti-evolution law would
bring down upon the state the same condemnation that the North had showered
upon Tennessee, T. T. Martin delivered a
speech decrying any subservience to the
North: "Go back to the fathers and mothers of Mississippi and tell them that because you could not face the scorn and
abuse of Bolsheviks and Anarchists and
Atheists and agnostics and their co-work-
ers, you turned their children over to a
teaching that God's Word is a tissue of
lies."[23] In a more sober vein James I. Fin-
ney, editor of the *Nashville Tennessean*,
observed of the anti-evolution legislation
in his state: "Thousands of intelligent
Tennesseans who realized the futility and
unwisdom of the law were either silenced
or became its defenders when the Civil
Liberties Union entered the combat . . .
It will remain on the statute books of
Tennessee until those who assail it retreat
from their position that belief in the fundamentals of the Christian religion is a
sign of mental weakness and bigotry."[24]
Thus ridicule, which made good copy for
northern writers, played a part in the
eruption of southern orthodoxy and became another of the many causes of the
fundamentalist controversy.

[23] Quoted in Mecklin, *My Quest for Freedom*, p.
247.
[24] *Literary Digest*, Aug. 29, 1931, p. 18.

English-born ANDREW F. SINCLAIR (b. 1935)
received his doctorate from Cambridge University
and since 1967 has been managing director of Lorrimer
publishing house. He previously served as Director
of Historical Studies for Churchill College, Cambridge,
and has lectured in American history at University
College, London. He has written two books on the
Twenties in America—*Prohibition: the Era of Excess*
(1962) and *The Available Man: the Life behind the
Masks of Warren Gamaliel Harding* (1965)—and is
the author of *The Emancipation of the American
Woman* (1970). Sinclair views prohibition as a swelling
of conservative prejudice, undermined when the
moderates deserted the movement after the war.
What similarities are there between the prohibition
psychology and Fundamentalist thought? Why did
both movements resort to legislation? Was prohibition
an attempt to preserve rural dogma?*

Andrew F. Sinclair

The Prohibition Impulse

Recent research on the nature of prejudice has made a momentous discovery. The cognitive processes of prejudiced people are different in general from the cognitive processes of tolerant people. In fact, a person's prejudice is not usually a particular attitude to a particular question; it is more often a whole pattern of thinking about the world. The prejudiced person is given to simple judgments in general, to assertions, to definite statements, to terms of black and white. Ambiguity is an evil to him because set truth is the good. He thinks in stereotypes, in rules, in truisms, in the traditional folkways of his environment. Such education as he receives merely gives him more reasons for his old beliefs. Indeed, he is the man who was found frequently in the dominant middle class of the small town, on the Western farms, and in the Southern shacks, where no complex clamor of urban life unsettled the mind and brain and eyes from the easy pairings of right and wrong. He is the man who was the backbone of the dry cause.

The Eighteenth Amendment could not have been passed without the support of the psychologically tolerant, made temporarily intolerant by the stress of war. But when the moderates deserted the drys in time of peace, the hard core of the movement was revealed. The main areas of prohibition sentiment were the areas where the Methodist and Baptist churches had their greatest strength. These were the areas that fathered the bigot crusade of the Ku Klux Klan, which supported prohibition, among other moral reforms. Although many sincere drys were not bigots at the beginning of the campaign for the Eighteenth Amendment, they became bigots or left the cause by the time of repeal. Prohibition, an extreme measure, forced its extremes on its supporters and its enemies. Its study becomes a study of social excess.

Although there were reasonable moral and economic and medical reasons for supporting prohibition, the drys themselves exploited many irrational motives within themselves and their followers. Among the leaders of the cause, there was hysteria in their passion to wean the human race from alcohol. There was what one leader of the Anti-Saloon League found in another, "an almost revengeful hatred of the liquor traffic . . . a dogmatic and consecrated prejudice against organized wrong." There was an element of sadism and undue persecution in the drys' legislative pursuit of the sinner, and in the flogging of prostitutes and bootleggers by the Ku Klux Klan. There was a thirst for power, which revealed itself in the savage struggles for position and prestige within the dry organizations, and in the sixteen-hour days worked year after year for no profit except self-satisfaction by such men as Wayne B. Wheeler, the great lobbyist of the dry cause. There was also a deliberate exploitation of prejudiced mentalities among their listeners by revivalist preachers

such as Billy Sunday. Above all, until the failure of the World League Against Alcoholism, there was a feeling that prohibition was a winning global crusade, and that those first on the wagon would be first in the promised land of earth and heaven.

Among the followers of prohibition, there were other blind motives. There was the release from tension offered by the crusade against wrong. One "chastened crusader" confessed after the Women's Crusade against the saloons in Ohio in 1873, "The Crusade was a daily dissipation from which it seemed impossible to tear myself. In the intervals at home I felt, as I can fancy the drinker does at the breaking down of a long spree." Allied with this release was an unreasoning fear of hard liquor, instilled by decades of revival sermons. As a female supporter of beer and wine wrote in 1929, "It is not love of whisky which makes real temperance impossible in this year of grace. It is the fear of it, the blinding, demoralizing terror felt by good people who have never tasted anything stronger than sweet communion wine." This terror drove the extreme drys into a stupid and obnoxious pursuit of the drinker during prohibition, which made the whole dry cause stink in the nostrils of the moderate. The Durant and Hearst prize contests for a solution to the prohibition problem revealed its distorted importance in the minds of certain drys and gave them wide publicity. One woman suggested that liquor law violators should be hung by the tongue beneath an airplane and carried over the United States. Another suggested that the government should distribute poison liquor through the bootleggers; she admitted that several hundred thousand Americans would die, but she thought that this cost was worth the proper enforcement of the dry law.

Others wanted to deport all aliens, exclude wets from all churches, force bootleggers to go to church every Sunday, forbid drinkers to marry, torture or whip or brand or sterilize or tattoo drinkers, place offenders in bottle-shaped cages in public squares, make them swallow two ounces of castor oil, and even execute the consumers of alcohol and their posterity to the fourth generation.

This extremism was only prevalent among a small group of the drys, but it was enough to damn all drys as fanatics. They were not so, although their spokesmen often were. Yet, living in a time before Freud and psychology were widely understood, they did not question their own motives. It was a time when "the figure of God was big in the hearts of men," and the drive of personal frustration was put down to divine guidance. Men were not aware of the subconscious motives which made them prohibitionists; but these motives were none the less real. Behind the crusade against the saloon lurked the tormented spirits of many people.

Freud's masterpiece, *Civilization and Its Discontents,* suggests some of the unconscious forces that drove on the drys. The childish, the immature, those who had least recovered from the ignorant certainties of youth sought consolation in an authoritarian crusade, in the same way that those who cannot bear life without a father often make a father of God. Refuge from the ambiguities and difficulties of modern life was, for many of the drys, only to be found in total immersion in clear-cut moral reform. The saloon was a sufficient Satan to become the scapegoat of the devil in man. Abolition of the saloon was interpreted by the prohibitionists as a personal victory over doubt and sin in their own lives. With a terrible faith in equality, the pro-hibitionists often wanted to suppress in society the sins they found in themselves. . . .

It was in this wish to extend their own repressions to all society that the drys felt themselves most free from their constant inward struggle. Indeed, they defended their attacks on the personal liberty of other men by stating that they were bringing these men personal liberty for the first time. According to one dry leader, personal liberty reached its highest expression where the strongest inhibitions were invoked and enforced. Moreover, personal liberty was only possible once prohibition had freed the slaves of alcohol. Of course, in reality the drys were trying to bring personal liberty to themselves, by externalizing their anguished struggles against their own weaknesses in their battle to reform the weaknesses of others. The conflict between conscience and lust, between superego and id, was transferred by the drys from their own bodies to the body politic of all America; and, in the ecstasy of that paranoia which Freud saw in all of us, they would have involved the whole earth.

Freud, whose own life was hard, considered intoxicants a great blessing in the human struggle for happiness and in the warding off of misery. . . . Freud saw that the moderate use of liquor was necessary for driven men, who could not find other interests or gratifications against the miseries of the world. The prohibitionists, however, presumed that a man who was denied the bottle would turn to the altar. They were wrong. They closed the saloons, but the churches did not fill. Luckily, drugs, radios, motion pictures, automobiles, proliferating societies, professional sports, paid holidays, and the relaxed sexual ethics of the flaming twenties provided new outlets for the libidos of deprived drinkers. Without these new outlets, the drys might have had to deal with a psychological explosion.

Yet extremism was not confined to the ranks of the drys. If the moderate drys were shamed by the excesses and motives of the extreme drys, so the moderate wets were damned by the millions of heavy drinkers and alcoholics on their side. If some prohibitionists were compulsive in their craving for water for everybody, some drinkers were even more compulsive in their craving for an excess of liquor for themselves. Alcoholics may suffer from many inadequacies —emotional immaturity, instability, infantilism, passivity, dependence, pathological jealousy, oral eroticism, latent homosexuality, isolation, narcissism, and masochism. People who possess such defects are not to be deprived of their liquor by respect for the law of the land. They need understanding, not prohibition, which merely drives them into drinking any murderous substitute for liquor rather than no liquor at all. For the compulsive drinker drinks because he is compulsive by nature, as is the fanatical reformer. To deprive the compulsive drinker of his drink does not cure him. He is merely forced into the search for substitutes. Equally, the prohibition of a reform to a reformer would not make him give up all reforms. He would merely turn his neuroses onto another brand of reform.

The real tragedy of the prohibitionist ideology was that it left no room for temperance. The dry crusade slipped slowly from a moderate remedy for obvious evils into a total cure-all for society. The creed of the dedicated dry would not admit the existence of the moderate drinker. By definition, all drinkers were bound to become alcoholics. The moral of the famous propaganda piece *Ten Nights in a Bar-Room* was that the first sip of beer always and inevitably led to a drunkard's grave. So believing, the Anti-Saloon League could not attract moderate support by allowing the sale of light wines and beers. National prohibition had to be total. Yet if prohibition had been confined to prohibition of ardent spirits, as the early nineteenth-century temperance associations had recommended, the Anti-Saloon League might have had the support of the brewers, the winegrowers, and the majority of the American people to this day. A survey conducted in 1946 in America showed that fewer than two-fifths of the adult population ever drank spirits, either regularly or intermittently.

In the early days of their counterattack, the brewers and distillers matched the hysteria of the drys in their denunciations. They accused the prohibitionists of being cranks and crackpots, "women with short hair and men with long hair." According to the wets, America was less threatened by the "gentlemanly vices" than by "perfidy and phariseeism in public and private life." Many men "marked the distinction between moderation and intemperance," and rich red blood, rather than ice water, flowed in their veins. . . .

The doctrine of prohibition appealed to the psychology of excess, both in its friends and in its foes. They could find only evil in each other. Extremes conjure up extremes. The fight against the devil carries another devil in its exaggerations. With a consecrated prejudice on the part of the drys opposed to an unenlightened self-interest on the part of the wets, there was little room left for compromise. Indeed, the drys were proud of their prejudice. It seemed to them a holy sentiment. With Robert Ingersoll, they did not believe that any person could contemplate the evils of drink "without being prejudiced against the liquor crime."

The extremes of dry psychology were well suited to white Southerners. They had a special use for prohibition. It offered them a moral refuge from their guilty fear of the Negro, as well as a method of controlling one of his means of self-assertion. Liquor sometimes gave the Negro the strength to repudiate his inferior status. It also encouraged him to loose his libido on white women, incited, so it was said, by the nudes on the labels of whisky bottles. Thus the Negro should be prevented from drinking alcohol. To a lesser degree, the same rule should be applied to white men, although this reform was not so urgent. Congressman Hobson, from Alabama, made this clear in the House of Representatives in 1914, while speaking on his resolution for a prohibition amendment to the Constitution. "Liquor will actually make a brute out of a negro, causing him to commit unnatural crimes. The effect is the same on the white man, though the white man being further evolved it takes longer time to reduce him to the same level."

In the same debate, Congressman Pou, of North Carolina, although he opposed Hobson's resolution on account of the sacred doctrine of states' rights, did not question the need for racial control. He reminded Congress gently that the South had been forced to take away the ballot from the Negro "as the adult takes the pistol from the hand of a child." Since the ballot and alcohol were the two means of assertion given to the Negro, they must be denied to him. By the time of the Hobson resolution, all the Southern states had discriminated against the Negro voter and all but two had adopted

prohibitory laws against liquor. The first measure had allowed the second. Congressman Quin, of Mississippi, stressed this in reference to the South. "Prohibition itself gained a foothold there and was made possible only after the restriction upon the suffrage of the negro." To Northern drys, even if the South was in the rout of democracy at the polling booth, it was in the van of reform at the saloon. If it denied the Fifteenth Amendment, it was rabid in support of the Eighteenth.

This paternalism among the responsible Southern leaders and the denial of the principle of equality was not confined to the white race. Professor Councill, the principal of the Negro school in Huntsville, Alabama, spoke out for the abolition of the saloon as the first step in the emancipation of his own race. . . . Booker T. Washington was of much the same opinion. Prohibition would be a blessing to the Negro people second only to the abolition of slavery. "Two-thirds of the mobs, lynchings, and burnings at the stake are the result of bad whisky drunk by bad black men and bad white men." Negro and white leaders could join together in the crusade against the saloon, which often incited the racial fears of the South to the pitch of murder.

Two other forces drove the Southerners towards prohibition. The first was patriotism. The South was once again the moral leader of the nation in this reform, and in this reform lay the chance of revenge. If the North had abolished chattel slavery in the South, the South would retaliate by abolishing rum slavery in the North. The second force was the monolithic structure of the Democratic party in the South. Traditionally, the Negroes voted Republican and the whites Democratic. The elimination of Negro ballots at the polls left the Democratic party solidly in control of Southern patronage. The only chance for the Republicans to regain some form of political power lay in the proper enfranchisement of the Negroes, which was impossible, or in the wresting of the moral leadership of the South from the Democrats. To do so, they had to find a popular cause which was both moral and an instrument of racial control. Prohibition was such a cause. Fear that the Republicans might seize the leadership of the prohibition movement, or that the Prohibition party, founded in 1869, might split the Democratic vote and let in the Republicans, drove the Democrats into the dry column in the South. Thus the anomaly of a party based on the wet cities of the North and the dry rural counties of the South was emphasized. The quarrel over prohibition brought into the open a deep fissure among the Democrats that made them ineffective as a party for a decade.

Other forces conspired to give alcohol a special position in the psyche of the South. Although white rural Southerners shared in the nationwide economic and moral drives toward prohibition, they also suffered from the peculiar compulsions given to them by their environment. In the Southern character, an overwhelming need to master the Negro was coupled with a split between Puritanism and hedonism. This split made the Southerner seek the forbidden as a necessary part of his greatest pleasure, while a sense of guilt drove him into dependence on the absolution of violence or of orgiastic religion. The ambivalent attitude of the Southern country white toward the Negro, his emotional cocktail of fear shaken up with lust, was also his attitude toward liquor. It is no coincidence that Mississippi, the most deeply rural of all states, is the last state in the Union to keep to the Southern trinity of official prohibition, heavy liquor consumption, and an occasional lynching. When Will Rogers commented that Mississippi would vote dry as long as the voters could stagger to the polls, he was too kind to mention that they would also lynch Negroes as long as they could stagger to the rope.

The drys deliberately exploited this darkness in the Southern mind. Fundamentalist religion often attracted large audiences by the very emphasis on vice and iniquity, violence and rape, which the mass media and the yellow press adopted in the twentieth century. An example can be taken from the work of the Reverend Wilbur Fisk Crafts. He was very influential, being president of the International Reform Bureau at Washington, a prolific writer and speaker, and a pastor at different times in the Methodist Episcopal, Congregational, and Presbyterian churches. His favorite sermon on prohibition began with a description of a man in seventeenth-century Bavaria who confessed on the rack that he had eaten thirteen children, after being changed into a wolf by the devil's girdle. The man was then sentenced to be put on the wheel and beheaded, once he had been pinched in twelve places on his body with red-hot irons. His dead body was burned, and his head was set for many years on a wooden wolf as a warning.

After this edifying start, the preacher continued,

So runs the old chronicle. Has it any parallel in present-day life? The next time you open your newspaper and read the scare heads describing the latest lynching horror in the black belt of the United States, ask yourself what devil's girdle has changed so many negroes into sensual hyenas. Remember that during the four years of the Civil War the whole white womanhood of the South, in the absence of husband and brother, in the death grapple of battle, was at the mercy of the black population of the plantations.

Yet there was no rape at that time. What, then, had changed the Negroes? Was it emancipation or education, or the possession of the suffrage? Or was it the fact, "which for all rational men is a sufficient answer," that 75 per cent of all liquor sales in the South Carolina dispensaries were to Negroes? Naturally, it was liquor which was the devil's girdle and brought about the punishment reserved for those who wore the devil's girdle. "The souls of the black men are poisoned with alcohol and their bodies in due course drenched in petroleum and burned."

Of course, lynching was only the extreme manifestation of the Southern urge to violence in the same way as hoggish drunkenness and ecstatic shakes were extreme reactions to the saloon and the revival meeting. There was a responsible and moderate leadership in the Deep South, composed of such people as Senator Oscar Underwood, of Alabama, who opposed prohibition and the excesses of his countrymen with conviction and dignity. But unfortunately, the very conditions which made the Western farms and small towns susceptible to the Manichaean doctrines of the drys were present in an exaggerated form in the South. There were few large cities. The hold of the primitive Methodist and Baptist churches and of the fundamentalist sects was widespread and powerful. Little industry existed below the Potomac. Conquest by the North and memories of Reconstruction lived on. And the cult of purity and white womanhood allied with the fact of miscegenation and Negro mistresses produced in the white Southerner a strange discrepancy between stressed morality and denied fact. In

this interval between ideal and reality, the cant of the drinker who voted dry flourished like a magnolia tree.

The South adopted prohibition to protect itself against its poor and its Negroes and its own sense of guilt. Those American missionaries who supported prohibition at home and abroad had like motives. The poor and the colored people of the earth were dangerous when drunk. Moreover, as the greed of Southern planters was held responsible for the existence of the Negro problem in the South, so the greed of white traders was usually held responsible for the corruption of the native races overseas. Early American imperialism imitated the European pattern of traders who corrupted the local people with rum and firearms and diseases, followed by clergymen who tried to save those people from that corruption. In America itself, the defeat of the red Indians had been made easy by their introduction to rum; once they had been defeated, they were immediately protected from the consequences of rum by the federal government.

A similar process took place in the Pacific islands. In 1901, Senator Henry Cabot Lodge had a resolution adopted by the Senate to forbid the sale by American traders of opium and alcohol to "aboriginal tribes and uncivilized races." These provisions were later extended to cover "uncivilized" elements in America itself and in its territories, such as Indians, Alaskans, the inhabitants of Hawaii, railroad workers, and immigrants at ports of entry.

The evil which the American missionaries were trying to eradicate was real enough. As they said, Christian nations were making ten drunkards to one Christian among backward peoples. Prohibition of rum traders was obviously a good

thing in those areas controlled by the colonial powers. But when the same paternal attitude was applied within the home ground of the colonial powers to "handle the hundreds of thousands of God's weak children, who are being ruined and destroyed through the oppressions of the liquor traffic," the missionaries ran into trouble. They could say with truth, "Let no one think we are neglecting saloons on our own shores in this crusade for the defense of native races at a distance." But the fact that the colonial power itself was often a democracy made this missionary attitude objectionable at home. No American workingman liked to be classified with those "uncivilized" peoples, whom he was taught to consider an inferior species. He also objected to the attitude of the missionary, who claimed to know what was good for labor better than labor knew itself. Moreover, there was a suspicious similarity between the views of the employers, who said that prohibition was good for the efficiency of workingmen, and those men of God, who said that prohibition was necessary for the salvation of their souls.

The idea of world-wide prohibition was contemporaneous with the idea of America as the Messiah of mankind and the Savior of the degenerate world. The ideology of salvation, which was once applied by middle-class reformers only to backward races and the American poor, was applied to the whole globe, after the First World War seemed to prove to many Americans that their country was the last refuge of peace and virtue. In addition, the spate of prohibition legislation adopted by the belligerent powers seemed to herald a world-wide prohibition revolution. Canada and Russia forbade liquor during the war; Britain and France and Germany severely regulated

liquor. The Moslem and Buddhist world was also officially under religious prohibition. In fact, over half the area of the earth seemed behind the dry banners, and that area was growing. It is small wonder that William Jennings Bryan could prophesy that "alcohol as a beverage has been indicted as a criminal, brought up to the bar of judgment, condemned, and executed. Our nation will be saloonless for evermore and will lead the world in the great crusade which will drive intoxicating liquor from the globe."

The mentality of war and the fantastic hopes of a millennial peace encouraged the drys' sense of international mission. As the leader of the Anti-Saloon League said to its assembled delegates in 1919, "The President said to make the world safe for democracy. Now, it is your business and mine, it is the business of the church of God, to make a democracy that is safe for the world, by making it intelligent and sober everywhere." The reason for converting the world was simple. It was the same reason, incidentally, that the Bolsheviks gave for insisting on the world-wide Communist revolution. As long as a dry America was surrounded by wet nations, or a Communist Russia by capitalist nations, neither prohibition nor Communism would be safe. How, in the opinion of the drys, could prohibition be enforced when the United States was bounded "on the north by hard liquor, on the south by liquor, on the west by rum and on the east by no limit"? The best hope of prohibition, like the best hope of communism, lay in the conquest of the world.

Of course, the drys saw themselves as the sworn enemies of the Bolsheviks and of communism. They said that they were the defenders of the law and the Constitution, where the Eighteenth Amendment was enshrined. But they did not mention their revolutionary destruction of the vast property interests of the liquor trade without compensation. There were further curious similarities between the Anti-Saloon League and the Bolshevik party. Both organizations were founded at much the same time. Both were small, successful, well-organized minority groups who knew what they wanted. Both exploited a condition of war to put themselves in power. Although the drys used propaganda while the Bolsheviks used revolutionary warfare, both used the methods most likely to succeed in their societies. Both groups expected through historical necessity to be the leaders of a global revolution in the habits of human society. The expectations of both groups were quickly disappointed. While Russia settled down under Stalin to "Socialism in one country," the United States settled down to prohibition in one country. Both revolutions failed in their immediate social objectives, although the names and the language of the Russian revolution lingered on.

But the analogy can be taken too far. The fact that the drys relied on the Christian churches and on democratic procedures limited their success. The methods of the World League Against Alcoholism could not be the methods of international subversion of the Comintern. When Bishop Cannon demanded of the Anti-Saloon League, "Shall It Live or Die?" and came to the conclusion that it should live to lead in the international crusade against alcohol, his suggested methods of conquest were the usual propaganda methods of the League. "It must carry

to every nation its testimony for Prohibition, by printed page, by cartoon, poster, in every language, and by trained workers and speakers who will be veritable apostles of Prohibition truth." That such a crusade was hardly likely to be effective in Mediterranean countries long used to drinking wine, did not deter the leaders of the League. For, as long as the crusade against liquor lasted at home and abroad, they kept their power and their jobs and their hopes and their satisfaction in the good fight well fought. It is the habit of revolutionaries never to be content with the limits of their gains, and of moral reformers rarely to accept less than the conversion of the human race.

The hidden urges behind dry leaders and white Southerners and foreign missionaries made them adopt prohibition as a panacea for themselves and for their fellow men. The dry cause brought them peace from their inner struggles and fears and guilt. They sought to extend this peace to races and classes which they considered inferior and eventually to the whole earth. The freedom of the globe from the evil of liquor would bring the condition of liberty for the first time to all mankind. In this battle for the good of all, the drys would use any means to win. For the liquor enemy was evil and could only be fought by evil. In their exploitation of the fears and weaknesses of their fellow Americans, the drys were guilty of many questionable methods, which could hardly be justified by the purity of their intentions.

JAMES W. PROTHRO (b. 1922) holds a Ph.D. in
political science from Princeton University. He
presently teaches at the University of North Carolina
and serves as Director of the Louis Harris Political
Data Center. Besides *The Dollar Decade: Business
Ideas in the 1920's* (1954), he is the author of *Negroes
and the New Southern Politics* (1966). Business
spokesmen of the Twenties, Prothro maintains,
categorically suggested that man's "nature could realize
its loftiest aspirations only in a materialistic heaven
on earth." Did the general public share this view? How
did the materialistic drive become ingrained in the
American mind? Have Americans characteristically
equated material success with progress?*

James W. Prothro

Material Success Glorified

Like any political theory, the political
ideas propagated in the name of American business are concerned with ideal
as well as reality, with life as it ought
to be as well as with life as it is. As one
might expect, the business conception
of the *summum bonum* and the means
toward its realization involves no abrupt
break with its theory of man's natural
capacity and of the external and internal
forces which help to mold him.

For Plato the *summum bonum* may
have been found in a mystical awareness
of the transcendental reality, for St.
Thomas it may have been in the realization of God's will, and for Marx it may
have been in the achievement of a Third
Realm on earth. But any such character-

ization of the highest good would constitute a discrete element in the structure of
business thought as it has been built thus
far. The *summum bonum* envisaged by
business leadership represents a much
more earth-bound type.

Aristotle, cited by at least one business
spokesman as a free-wheeling exponent
of private enterprise, felt that the highest
good could be experienced only by an
individual with a well-ordered soul. For
him, one who achieved the desired virtue
would possess a moderate amount of the
external objects necessary for comfort,
a healthy body, and, most important,
the goods of the soul.

Rather than relying on the Aristotelian
view of such an important subject as this,

*From James W. Prothro, *The Dollar Decade: Business Ideas of the 1920's* (Baton Rouge: Louisiana
State University Press, 1954), pp. 60–76. Reprinted without footnotes by permission.

45

however, business leaders preferred to go their own way. The three levels of goods Aristotle thought necessary to the good life are all subsumed in the theory of the National Association of Manufacturers and the Chamber of Commerce under what was to Aristotle the most subsidiary of man's needs, the goods of an external, mundane sort. They become so important in the business theory as to constitute almost an exclusive point of focus for man's energies and aspirations. And the moderate quantity of these goods which Aristotle would have one seek is multiplied manifold in keeping with their increased qualitative importance.

William Feather enthusiastically spoke for the business community in picturing the virtues of an economic sort of *summum bonum.* Man would find, and in the United States had largely found, the good life through the accumulation of economic goods which, writ large, spelled The Good that all sought. Man's nature could realize its loftiest aspirations only in a materialistic heaven on earth.

This business ideal was one which early philosophers could not have shared because it was uniquely American. "I think there is a specific central idea in every 100 per cent American, and that it is the cause of our amazing prosperity, and the reason for our inability to accept European forms and customs," Feather began. "Because the 100 per cent American is different from any other animal on the face of the earth he has no real interest in foreign art, and because his own artists have failed to understand Americanism, enthusiasm for native art in this country has never been more than lukewarm."

What was the origin of this American vision of the *summum bonum* which it is impossible for such as artists and for-

eigners to appreciate? "Birth was given to the American idea the year the steam engine was invented. The Declaration of Independence postulated freedom and equality of opportunity. The steam engine furnished man with a new source of energy—uncarnate instead of carnate."

Spawned by a British inventor, the uniquely American idea needed only a proper political climate to offer every 100 per cent American a chance to realize the good life. This good life is unquestionably economic in content. "With the steam engine it was possible to found a civilization on prosperity. The 100 per cent American is saturated with the idea of prosperity and equality."

Surrounded by material blessings, the American is not attracted to the spurious goals of foreigners, whether socialistic or Christian in content. As Feather observes, "With a full belly and a warm hut man no longer needs to be drugged by socialism and personal salvation; and the art and literature produced under the patronage of kings and potentates." Having experienced the exaltation of the good life, "he demands something new, something that expresses his release from economic oppression, hunger, cold, and weariness."

That there are other worthy values in addition to the material, business spokesmen would not deny. But the false note in other theories is struck by the fact that they try to elevate these lesser ends above the material. In truth, however, it is impossible to conceive of any values except in terms of the highest good, which is material.

Just as the worth of a man was found to be measurable only in material units, so is the quality of an abstract value measurable only in the same terms. Charles N. Fay emphatically underlines this point. "Certainly, if humanity is to pro-

gress, its gain must be intellectual and spiritual as well as material," he concedes. "Yet how do we measure intellectual progress," he asks, "if not by schools and universities? How do we measure spiritual progress; if not by churches and charities, setting up standards of character, ethics and morals?"

However qualitative the concept, then, it is susceptible to evaluation only in a quantitative fashion. There are those who think differently, of course, but they represent outmoded and foreign points of view. That America had escaped such a distorted outlook was beyond dispute. "No place is reserved in the United States for European eighteenth century ideas. We don't understand them. We have no beggars, no meek and lowly, no cow-like women, no starved children."

On the contrary, the acclimated resident of the New World had glimpsed the highest good. And he hoped to realize it in a more substantial fashion than could be expected from that fleeting experience of the ultimate good which Plato held out as the goal. Already Feather could observe with satisfaction, "We are rich, fat, arrogant, superior." The only remaining need was for the world of literature to recognize the peculiar quality of the American ideal. "Why doesn't someone interpret us as we really are . . . ," ran the refrain of business' lament.

The request for an interpretation of the good life as it had begun to unfold in America alone was met from several quarters. Perhaps the most widely read interpretation of the American *summum bonum* was offered by Sinclair Lewis under the familiar title *Babbitt*. While this analysis met the request of American business, it did not meet its needs. Lewis could not be said to have failed in the objective of depicting the 100 per cent American as "rich, fat, arrogant, supe-

rior," but the patronizing contempt of the author was too thinly veiled to be lost on the business community.

Business spokesmen naturally objected to the caricature quality of the portrait, but they quickly identified it as their own, however distorted the features. Despite the cynicism and scorn attached to the likeness, they unhesitatingly embraced the core of true values that it revealed and rushed to their defense.

An editorial in *Nation's Business* entitled "Dare To Be a Babbitt!" laid down the first salvo in what was to be a sustained campaign in defense of Babbittry. "Good Rotarians who live orderly lives, and save money, and go to church, and play golf, and send their children to school quake when some advanced thinker hurls at them the damning word 'Babbitt.'"

This feeling of vulnerability the editorialist considered completely uncalled for. Put in proper perspective, the values of Babbitt came close to realizing the *summum bonum* of the business community. "Was Babbitt so evil a thing? Should we despise him for his pride in his real-estate business, his membership in the Zenith Boosters' Club and the Zenith Chamber of Commerce, his simple joy in the conveniences of his life and his home? His house and his manners may have suffered from over-standardization, but his was a kindly soul with an eagerness to work and play with his fellow-men."

Surely these are virtues rather than proper targets for derision. "Would not the world be better for more Babbitts and fewer of those who cry, 'Babbitt'?" To the staff of *Nation's Business* the answer was as obvious as it must have been to all of their readers. "Every day we read of some business man who has given lavishly to make life better for his fellows," they wrote with assurance. "Just last month *Nation's Business* told of how George

Eastman tackled the job of giving. . . .
But Mr. Eastman belongs to the Chamber
of Commerce. He may even be a Kiwa-
nian or a Civitan. He's a Babbitt! Let's
take his money and jeer at him!"

As a number of business spokesmen
pointed out in describing the motives of
the inferior, envy may often find expression in the condemnation of one's betters.
Aware of the rancorous jealousy of those
less fortunate, business leaders were more
tolerant than might have been expected.
The perverse criticisms of uncompre-
hending foreigners and native artists at
least served the function of pointing up
the *summum bonum* and stimulating
business spokesmen to identify it.

The unkind treatment by the French
critic André Siegfried of what he conceived to be America's obsession with
materialism served this function admira-
bly. Merle Thorpe unhesitatingly turned
to counterattack with a series of rhetorical
questions as his weapons: "Is it then so
discreditable a thing to be prosperous?
To make ends meet, to desire greater
comforts and conveniences, to labor hard
and acquire them? Must a man be belly-
hungry before he can be mind and soul
hungry? Is it a virtue to be work-less and
hopeless?"

Indictments of business values because
of their dedication to an economic type of
summum bonum were thus met with a
demurrer. What point was there in deny-
ing their materialism when it was an
orientation shared by all true Americans?
Against the lampooning involved in the
portrayal of Babbitt was placed evidence,
not to contradict the portrait but to show
that the business elite spread the value
in question by sharing their goods with
others. With the whole people "saturated
with the idea of prosperity" the foreigner
who observed as much could be met with
cheerful assent.

It was not only in their polemic writings
that business spokesmen faced the question of identifying and justifying the
type of *summum bonum* they envisaged.
Charles N. Fay carefully reflected on the
different types of goals that might represent man's *summum bonum* and came to
the conclusion that the highest good must
be economic. This proposition was veri-
fied whether one argued the case on *a
priori* or pragmatic grounds.

If the *summum bonum* represents the
highest good toward which man can aspire, it must arise from a projection of the
best in man's nature. Since man's most
deep-rooted and laudable characteristic
is his innate selfishness and since that
selfishness seeks economic expression,
man's *summum bonum* can be conceived
only in an economic form. Thus Fay
firmly grounds his argument in the nature of human motivations: ". . . history
shows that the prime motive of capitalism
—namely, *selfishness,*—merely reflects
the conviction, *inborn in every living
creature,* that *it is his natural right to
keep, own and control whatever he himself has made, saved, thought out, bought
or fought for;* a conviction which works
out broadly not only for *justice* to the
individual, but to the common good of
all."

Here Fay was arguing from original
principles with the assurance of a lat-
ter-day John Locke. And insofar as he
departs from the Lockean tradition, it
is to undertake the difficult task of
elevating property to the status of an
even more all-encompassing end than
Locke could contemplate. "*Original production* had to determine *original ownership,* before laws recognizing right of
ownership—that is, codes of justice or
morals—could be framed to maintain
that right. In short, wealth must come,
and always did come, *first in point of*

time! Law, morals, education, and even religion, at least as we practice them, *have always evolved upward as consequents,* not precedents of property." If wealth antedates not merely government but morals, education, and religion as well, it may be deemed to represent man's highest and most permanent end.

Turning from *a priori* reasoning to a more pragmatic approach, one arrives at the same conclusion. Merle Thorpe's question—"Is it a virtue to be work-less and hopeless?"—is easily answered by a brief look at history. "Indeed, if one asks the rather ungracious question, *what have unselfish poverty and asceticism actually done for the greatest good of the greatest number,* or how far have they practically contributed to the evolution upward of the human race—which certainly began long before history and the dawn of civilization, and which still goes on,—one must reluctantly own that their usefulness, *as actual factors* in the progress of humanity, cannot be established nearly as well as that of capitalism."

Where has mankind come closest to realizing the highest good? Quite evidently it is where he has come closest to achieving the maximum saturation with materialism. "Compare, if you will, Darkest Africa today, where there are no capitalists, no railways, banks or factories—or Soviet Russia, where a robber state has murdered them,—or India and China, where they are slowly evolving—or South America and South Eastern Europe, where they are coming along faster—with Germany, France or England; especially with our own fortunate America."

One finds from such a survey that not only the highest good but subsidiary values are directly dependent on material satisfaction. "Have not peace and plenty, respect for life, liberty and law, the virtues of toleration and of stable self-government—have not all these blessings, in all history, gone hand-in-hand with industry, thrift and wealth, both general and individual?"

If every type of human desideratum is found, historically, only as a concomitant of materialism, one must conclude that all values stem directly from the material. "Is it, therefore, going too far to assert," Fay asks, "that *these happy conditions exist in our beloved country because of our wealth?*" It is only logical to concede that, insofar as man achieves his greatest goal, the lesser ends in his hierarchy of values will come to him automatically.

To the extent that he realizes the highest good, man should become a more estimable creature. And twentieth century America had come closest to attaining the *summum bonum* of business. Glen Buck, the business publicist, explained that the United States was in the process of becoming "the richest nation in history." For those with discernment this could only mean that man himself was being elevated. As Buck put it, ". . . in what process a keener, cleaner manhood has been developed, else the remarkable pace would not have been possible."

As important as the type of end which man envisions is the means through which that goal may be approached. The *summum bonum* could be sought for Plato only through contemplation, for St. Thomas through salvation, and for Marx through the act of revolution. In each case the means is closely related to the end. And since the highest good is never easy to realize, the means itself becomes the immediate end. Indeed, for the less fortunate it must remain the ultimate goal.

Although the *summum bonum* of American business is found in materialism, one does not achieve the good life by abandoning himself immediately or completely to its charms. The path to the *summum bonum* is by no means so easy. Perhaps because the United States was so close to making the good life available to all during the 1920's, the less perceptive were in danger of forgetting this truth and losing themselves in premature enjoyment of a bastard *summum bonum.*

President Edgerton warned, "It is time for America to awake from its dream that an eternal holiday is the natural fruit of material prosperity, and to reaffirm its devotion to those principles and laws of life to the conformity with which we owe all of our national greatness."

What is the key to our national greatness? It unquestionably lies in the American tradition of hard and unstinting work. Edgerton accordingly follows his admonition with the observation, "I am for everything that will make work happier, but against everything that will further subordinate its importance in the program of life."

The road to the *summum bonum* may not be easy, then, but at least it is clear to all who have not been dazzled by that portion already traversed. If it constitutes the only means through which the *summum bonum* can be realized, work must be considered the most praiseworthy activity of man just as material greatness is his loftiest end. A. C. Bedford, a leader in the oil industry, revealed to Standard Oil employees that work was of more fundamental importance than love, learning, religion, or patriotism: ". . . even admitting the beauty, the charm, the inspiration and the greatness of these four qualities, none of them could be put into effective execution without work." . . .

As the exclusive means to man's highest end, work becomes sanctified itself. "There is a great truth in that old law: 'Six days shalt thou labor,'" one company

president observes. "Let us do it and be thankful for the privilege." Sanctified by its direct relation to the *summum bonum,* work may be considered man's most worthwhile immediate goal. The National Association of Manufacturers committee on industrial betterment, health and safety reflected such an appreciation of the merits of honest toil by reporting in 1920: "What this country now needs is one of our war drives—a national campaign for industriousness, thrift and common sense. A work slacker is no better than a soldier slacker." If work offers the only route to man's highest good, it should certainly be ranked as high as a willingness to fight for one's nation.

Work, like many terms in popular usage, could be referred to without careful definition. Even when one of the most respected of business leaders, Judge E. H. Gary, endeavored to define the term for the benefit of a Senate committee, he fell somewhat short of precision. "It is hard work to work hard whatever one does," Judge Gary began, "and to the extent one does work hard he, of course, is doing hard work. That is perfectly evident." Whatever this definition may have lacked in precision was more than compensated for by respect for the taxing quality of work. . . .

In 1920 the members of the National Association of Manufacturers readily responded to this interpretation. The nation's immigration policy, Louis Marshall submitted, should recognize that an applicant would make a far better American through willingness to labor than through the pursuit of literary effort or ideological niceties. "The fact that a man or woman cannot read or write—the so-called literacy test—to my mind is simple nonsense. (Applause.) The worst immigrants that have come to the United States have been men who are able to read and write in half a dozen different languages. (Applause.) The entire complement of the Soviet ark which sailed from New York a few months ago, consisted of literary people. (Laughter and applause.)"

In contrast to the subversive character of the literary type are the sturdy virtues of the man able to accept, if not to read, business road signs to the *summum bonum.* "The men who work in our shops, upon our railroads, in our factories, at our furnaces, in our mines, are useful men, not because they can read forty words in Bulgarian or Greek or Syrian, but because of their brawn and the disposition to be useful members of society. (Applause.) And yet Congress has deliberately placed upon our statute books a regulation which would keep out of the United States from thirty to thirty-five per cent of those who have heretofore come here and have performed useful service for their employers, for themselves and for their country. . . ."

If even the crudest sort of work constitutes an edifying experience, the same type of activity at a higher level may issue in the highest good. The work of the elite is doubly ennobling because it exposes not only the elite itself but the masses as well to the benefits of labor. Charles N. Fay explains that *"actually the most beneficent of all"* activities *"is for the strong man to create and save wealth, —and so to use it as to give many weaker men the certainty of self support in honorable toil:* offering *not charity, but wages for work well done. . . ."*

He who works assiduously enough to acquire wealth, then, has achieved greatness. Citing the pioneer figures in the oil industry as examples of men who had achieved such true greatness, A. C. Bedford concluded, "If one becomes a producer, one should also become a

money-maker, and provided he gets wealth honestly, I think such a man has every right to be considered great."

Spokesmen for the business community conceive of the *summum bonum* in an economic form and as approachable only through the avenue of hard work. An important remaining aspect of the problem is whether the *summum bonum* is considered possible of realization or should be regarded as a permanent goal the full substance of which can never be grasped. When men such as the leaders in the oil industry are said to have achieved true greatness, does this mean that they have tasted the highest good in its full flavor or simply that they have more nearly realized it than any of their fellows?

For the masses this problem assumes a peculiar form. Since they are inferior by definition, the *summum bonum* must be beyond their reach by the same token. But it will be remembered that the highest good of the unfit is often found in that which is only the means to the infinitely loftier goal of the fit. If they are willing to accept work as the highest good available, although it is only the avenue to the highest good in an absolute sense, it would appear that they could reasonably expect to achieve their highest end. It develops, however, that the realization of the *summum bonum* even in this relative sense is never complete.

While Dr. Gus W. Dyer is at his best in extolling the value of work as a goal for the masses, he lays equal stress on the fact that one's work should arise from freedom of access to different kinds of employment. "The most sacred right and privilege that American democracy guarantees to the American citizen is the right to work anywhere under the American flag without fear and without molestation, and the right to sell the products of his labor, or sell his labor, or buy the products of the labor of others on an open market, absolutely unrestricted at the best possible prices." So important does Dr. Dyer consider the mobility in employment implied in this statement that he avers, "It is the guarantee of this right and privilege that chiefly distinguishes a civilized country from a barbarous country."

Thus it is not merely work but the freedom to choose their work that is most important for the masses. This emphasis results from the fact that, while the *summum bonum* of the unfit lies in work, it is found not in labor alone but in the process of rising to higher levels of work. Even at the lowest level there can be no complete achievement of the *summum bonum;* it comes not from the achievement of any given status but from unending progress in status.

The masses should be dedicated to work, but even they can legitimately aspire to rise above certain forms of labor. William Feather attests to this fact by asserting that "the 100 per cent American realizes that he can unload all drudgery on machinery, and thereby achieve universal prosperity exceeding the dream of the most moony Bolshevist." This is not to contradict the idea of the importance of arduous labor; it is simply to suggest that the American will seek his highest good by progressing to more elevated forms of equally hard work.

The Honorable Walter E. Edge, speaking on the basis of his wide business experience rather than as a politician, pointed up this distinction for the benefit of the National Association of Manufacturers in 1920. Senator Edge made it clear to his listeners that the average American had raised himself above the lowest forms of physical effort. "America needs common-labor men for its fields and its facto-ries, for its mines and its hundreds of other circles of common labor. Through facing death in the great war the American youth and man sees the true standard of his own value, higher than in other years he had realized." What does this new recognition of his own value mean in practice? "Instead of plying a pick and shovel on a railroad right of way, he now knows he is fitted for better things, and, indeed, that he can be of more value to the world as captain or boss of the right-of-way men than he could at the business end of a spade."

Although recognizing the dignity of labor, Senator Edge was fully convinced that in raising himself above common labor the average individual was moving toward the good. "In short," he submitted, "the American man and youth has found himself. He has 'raised himself on stepping stones of his dead self to higher things.' And I cannot imagine his retrogressing and degenerating to his former and lower estate. Not that for a moment I would deprecate the value and even the dignity of manual labor; but, there are grades and strata of labor above whose level the American working-man stands. The American working-man is not to be condemned for developing 'a swelled head'; he is to be felicitated on stepping up to a higher personal standard."

Progress to higher levels of work may fall far short of the grandiose material achievements envisaged in the *summum bonum* of the business community, but it at least gives to the masses the feeling that they are on the same path as the elite, and it represents in itself a worthy ideal for ordinary men. Even foreigners brought to the United States for the specific purpose of performing the necessary common labor will catch the gleam of this lesser good available to all Americans.

With native Americans already on the path of progress, "men and women must be found to perform the more elemental work of all kinds on which Americans formerly were engaged. . . . The average foreigner, such as comes to our shores, is used to hard work, and all he needs is the guidance which will be furnished by Americans who have had the experience and served their apprenticeship in the elemental phases of work. As he works, of course, he will conceive ambition for advancement, and the struggle for attainment of worthy ambitions is one of the greatest factors in the ultimate production of worthy American citizens."

With all their limitations, the masses, both foreign and native-born, are dissatisfied with a static condition. Incapable of achieving the *summum bonum* in its true sense, they find what is for them the highest good in a continuous process of progress to higher grades of work. Work they never escape. On the contrary, it is an essential part of their highest goal. But they seek, in addition to the assurance of work, the chance to enjoy the satisfactions of progress.

When business spokesmen turn from the masses to the elite, they turn from a relative to an absolute conception of the *summum bonum*. These are the few who are perceptive enough to see beyond mere means to the true *summum bonum* of complete saturation with material achievements. If their goal is infinitely loftier, however, so were their capabilities found to be infinitely superior. Is there any greater possibility at this level that the highest good may be grasped and savored in a final and absolute sense?

At least in respect to this one problem the many and the few are held by the business theory to have something in common. However successful, the few are always able to find new goals. By virtue of their superior breadth of vision, it is even more out of the question for them than for the many to achieve complete satisfaction. Berton Braley, versifier for *Nation's Business,* underlines the economic content of the *summum bonum* and at the same time catches the spirit of an insatiable quest for bigger and better things:

Bill Babbitt is a hustler,
  A regular go-getter,
And when he's caught the thing he sought
  He goes for something better!

So when he's wanting money
  He does his best to make it.
(He makes no bluff to hate the stuff
  While being glad to take it).

In this unending process of achievement man finds as great a satisfaction as is destined for him. No one prize will imbue the able individual with a sense of final achievement; it is in the process of progress from one material goal to another that he realizes the *summum bonum*. It was Babbitt's inability to escape from this great truth that was largely responsible for bringing the business community to his defense. . . .

The elite naturally takes unashamed pride with Babbitt in material accomplishment, but it finds no complete satisfaction even here. Each success merely whets one's ambition and suggests new goals to be pursued. Charles M. Schwab offers categorical testimony on this point: "No first rate American business man is ever satisfied with what he accomplishes. He is always straining for the unattainable."

The highest good may be approached, then, but never fully grasped. Insofar as one has realized the *summum bonum* in part, he is impelled to continue unabated toward an ever greater, but never complete, realization. William Feather very logically concludes from this that "the 100 percent American dies in harness."

That man should find his good in material progress is a perfectly natural—indeed, an inevitable—result of his nature. The Deity itself defined man's goals in the process of determining his nature. Charles N. Fay submits in this connection that the "evolution upward of humanity must have been . . . the *intent* of the Creator of all things; in implanting deep in human nature the mighty motive of selfishness, and the constructive assertion of the right of private property." . . .

The complete picture of man's *summum bonum* offered in the political ideas of organized business fits logically with its earlier analysis of human nature from the point of view of its capacity, determinants, and motivations. Man had already been revealed as a creature highly unequal in endowments, whose nature could not be positively molded by any external forces except those to which his innate capacities automatically exposed him, and whose motivations were as unalterably selfish in nature as they were economic in content.

What would constitute an appropriate end for such a being? Few beneficiaries of the Amazing Decade could argue with the fact that his highest good must necessarily be economic in content. That it should be susceptible to approach only by way of hard work and that it could probably never be realized in a manner that would sate man's selfish ambitions appears to follow with equal congruity.

The minimum requisites for man's happiness, then, are "a full belly and a warm hut." These are not essential because, as Aristotle thought, they would free the individual from concern with material matters and allow him to concentrate on higher ends. On the contrary, they are important because they mean that man "no longer needs to be drugged" by the opiates of "socialism and personal salvation" or by the palliatives found in the art and literature of nonmaterialistic cultures. With these physical essentials, man has no reason to seek escape from reality and can focus all his energies on greater material achievements. Any nonmaterial values that are worthwhile will come to him automatically in the process.

Given a properly materialistic culture, man will realize that his *summum bonum* lies in the "greater comforts and conveniences" which Merle Thorpe extolled. And, if he is true to his nature, he will "labor hard and acquire them." In the temporary satisfaction of achievement, ever loftier dreams of material success will come to him. If he is among the able few, he will eventually appreciate the fact that his goal is the more precious because it is unattainable in any complete sense.

The economic content of this theory lends it a pronounced note of Marxism. Law, morals, education, and religion are all unveiled by the business theory as well as by Marx as "consequents, not precedents of property." And the Marxian view of life as conflict is matched by the business view of life as "the struggle for attainment of worthy ambitions."

But if this is Marxian, it must be called "inverted Marxism." For Marx the condition of struggle under economic compulsions represents the kingdom of darkness from which man must break, by act of revolution against the bourgeoisie, into a classless and propertyless kingdom of light. But in the business theory, it will be remembered, man began in a classless and propertyless regime and broke from it, by act of revolution against God, into a class-stratified and propertied kingdom of light. The effect of economic struggle is accordingly antithetical in the two systems. Rather than degrading man into a hopeless and miserable proletariat, the economic determinism envisaged by business spokesmen produces "a keener, cleaner manhood."

And the improvement of the species through universal saturation with the idea of prosperity had gone further in the United States than anywhere else. Not only could the 100 per cent American of the twentieth century look down on foreign values, but he had progressed so prodigiously that he could well consider himself more advanced than almost any American of earlier generations. Thus, the business theory would hold that

Thomas Jefferson, dying heavily in debt, must be judged a failure so far as the pursuit of the *summum bonum* is concerned.

Either because his values were misdirected or as a compensatory substitute for material success, Jefferson asked to have enscribed on his tombstone a record of nonmaterial achievement. One could undoubtedly find some solace in the thought that he was the author of the Declaration of Independence, the sponsor of the Virginia Statute of Religious Toleration, and the founder of the University of Virginia. But the 100 per cent American, insist the spokesmen of business, "desires no monument other than his works as a producer."

After receiving a doctorate from Radcliffe, CAROLINE F. WARE (b. 1889) taught history at Vassar for nearly a decade. Since then she has enjoyed a distinguished career both in teaching and government service. From 1945 until 1961 she was Professor of Social Work at Howard University and since then has served as a technical assistance expert to the United Nations. Her book *Greenwich Village, 1920–1930* (1935) is recognized as the classic study of the bohemian movement in America. Her treatment of the subject is balanced and considered, emphasizing the differences in the Villagers' background and attitudes. To what extent were the bohemians alienated from middle class American values? What positive attitudes did the Villagers hold?*

Caroline F. Ware

Bourgeois Values Scorned

During these years, the Village acted as a magnet which drew to it a wide variety of people with one quality in common, their repudiation of the social standards of the communities in which they had been reared. Here gathered in these years a whole range of individuals who had abandoned their home pattern in protest against its hollowness or its dominance, and had set out to make for themselves individually civilized lives according to their own conceptions. They had found the traditional Anglo-Protestant values inapplicable and the money drive offensive. In the Village, some sought to discover other positive values upon which to reconstruct a social system in America; many carried on those activities, espe-cially artistic, which had little or no place in a civilization dominated either by the remains of the Calvinist ethic or by the purely acquisitive impulse; an increasing proportion simply sought escape, and brought with them little except negative values, throwing over more or less completely whatever smacked of "Puritanism" or "Babbittry"; the more serious sought some compromise which would enable them to avoid the features which they did not like, but to retain those which they consciously or unconsciously cherished.

The Village was not the only place where those who repudiated their traditions took refuge during these years. Although it was the most notorious of such places, its counterpart could be found in

Chicago, San Francisco, and other large cities, and elsewhere in New York. Its notoriety did not make it unique, but only made it an advantageous point from which to observe the disintegration of old American culture in the post-War years in an acute, and, therefore, clearly visible form.

The Villager population, in 1930 and the years preceding it, included at one end of the scale those who cherished old American values, but found them so lost or submerged in the bourgeois world that they took refuge from the pressures of that world and sought the opportunity to re-create the old values in their own lives. At the other extreme were those who threw over altogether both the American and the bourgeois patterns and sought complete freedom, defiance, or escape in flight to Greenwich Village. In between these two elements was the great mass of Village residents whose repudiation of their background was only partial and who consequently presented various conflict situations where that which they had retained interfered with that which they had cast aside. The first of these groups was the one which discovered the Village in its early, unsung days. The second gave it its reputation. The third made up by 1930 the largest element in its Villager population. Though these groups were not completely separated from each other, and lines between them were not hard and clear, they presented essentially distinct forms of adaptation and associated in groups which roughly followed these lines. All, however, shared certain basic common qualities which distinguished them both from their neighbors in that other social world and from their home communities—namely, a disregard for money values and for prestige based on either income or conspicuous expenditure, an awareness of some sort

of cultural values, and tolerance of unconventional conduct even when their own habits were more constrained.

Unconventionality, especially in the matter of sex, was taken for granted, and attitudes ranged from tolerance of experimentation to approval rather than from condemnation to tolerance. The sober superintendents of "respectable" apartment houses made no bones about enumerating "girls and their fellers" among the occupants of their houses when trying to rent an apartment to a middle aged lady. Villagers of conventional tastes were distinctly on the defensive in explaining to the interviewer that "all the people in Greenwich Village aren't the kind that you expect to find. There are plenty of ordinary respectable people like us." No one felt called upon to be on the defensive about the opposite type of conduct.

All types of Villagers were intensely individualistic in both their social relations and their point of view. Their social contacts were confined to more or less purposeful relations with those who had common interests. Independent of virtually all institutions and scorning the joining habit, taking full advantage of both the selectiveness and the anonymity which the city offered, they avoided the usual casual contacts with family, neighbors, or members of the same economic or social class and the relations growing out of institutional connections. Instead, they maintained individual ties with friends scattered all over the city. If they had professional or artistic interests, these were apt to furnish a basis for their social life. The pursuit of an avocation or common tastes in recreation brought others together.

It was not always easy or possible to make connections with those of common interests. In the early days of the Village, when numbers were few and most Villagers had common interests in art or social reform, it had been possible for newcomers to find their way, chiefly via eating-houses, into congenial company. As more people and more different types came in, newcomers could no longer count on falling in with congenial company. Yet at each stage in the Village's history some one group was identified with the locality and offered easy contacts to newcomers. In 1930, it was the pseudo-bohemians and especially the Lesbians, into whose group it was easily possible for strangers to find their way.

To trace the modification of traditional American behavior patterns during these years by means of any sort of statistical sample of Villagers would be impossible, because the essence of their effort at adjustment was its extreme individualism. Whereas among the other elements in the community it was usually possible to reconstruct the essentials of their social attitudes from a knowledge of certain parts, many of the Villagers had gone so far in their repudiation that their values followed no pattern. In the case of the young people in whom the Village abounded, moreover, there was no way of predicting their future, and their Village life was difficult to analyze without a knowledge of whether they would return to their small home communities, settle down to a bourgeois existence in the suburbs, make some successful form of city adaptation, or drift from bar to bar for the rest of their lives. As this community, like other city neighborhoods, furnished a refuge for many persons who were psychologically mal-adapted, a heavy overlay of psychological problems frequently obscured the sociological implications of the position and attitudes of many Villagers.

It was possible, however, to block out the main types of adaptation and repudia-tion and to describe the groups which fell within those types. The members of the groups did not remain constant, but the types endured, represented by some old and some new individuals from year to year. Succeeding groups with their different sorts of reactions in turn imparted their reputation to the Village as its dominant element, at least in the eyes of the outside world. In 1930, all these groups were still present, the earlier represented either by remnants of the personnel which had constituted the original groups or by newcomers of the same type as those who had left. The same range of types found in 1930, moreover, had been present in the years before, differing only in their relative numerical strength and in some of the specific attitudes which characterized them.

As the backflow to the Village, increased, however, the relative prominence of different types changed. The first group of Villagers had been made up of individuals of exceptional independence, who had faced social problems with earnestness and had sought positive solutions. When the community had come to contain a large proportion of persons of ordinary caliber whose position reflected the social situations from which they had come more than the personal quality of the individuals, the negative desire to escape took the place of any positive quest, and social earnestness gave way to a drifting attitude. At the same time, the actual expression of repudiation became more extreme as the conduct which had constituted social defiance at one time became commonplace a few years later. The disappearance of smoking as an issue, the spread of drinking, and the passing on from free love to homosexuality were only the more obvious of the manifestations which were successively adopted to mark the outposts of revolt.

Art, sex, and a disdain for the pursuit of wealth were the key points by which it was possible to test the nature and the degree of departure from the old American tradition.

Interest in money-making for its own sake and in the world of business was rare among all types of Villagers. Though those who refused to compromise with the materialistic world even to the point of earning a living were a small minority, even a sample of distinctly conservative Villager men showed sixteen per cent never looking at the financial section of the newspaper, in contrast to a corresponding group of townspeople in similar occupations where only two per cent failed to follow the financial news.

Neither in the old American culture pattern nor in that dominated by bourgeois values had either artist or writer an integral place. Although it was the part of cultivation to know the works of classical writers, it was not in the genteel tradition to be an artist or a writer by profession, particularly either a struggling or an experimental one who was not a success on the money-making front and who did not accept the dictates of respectable taste. Except for the circumstances which produced the Concord group in the years before the Civil War, artist and writer had found the American environment thoroughly uncongenial and, in the absence of social status or a critical audience, they had either been driven, like Henry James, to seek expatriation or to retire into themselves like Emily Dickinson. Those who made much of art were, by the mere fact of this emphasis, registering a repudiation of traditional attitudes. In addition, the Village artists departed conspicuously from those forms of art expression which were acceptable to the American community. The attack on the genteel tradition, led by the genuine artists, became a secondary symbol of the scorn in which the staid world was held, and those whose art registered their social attitude rather than their talent felt compelled to violate all the established rules of versification, punctuation, or composition.

Art, moreover, served a purpose which no other form of repudiation filled in that it offered positive as well as negative values, not simply the discarding of an empty or unacceptable social pattern, but a way of life in itself. And upon this fact rested its relation to the many groups in the Village, none of whom possessed any coherent alternative to the social pattern which they more or less vigorously despised. It was to art as a way of life that all turned, either as a means of satisfying themselves or of giving themselves status in a society in which art was the one recognized form of divergence. Hence, practically all groups in one way or another, even though they had no artistic capacities themselves, attempted to justify themselves to themselves and to society in some artistic or literary terms or longed to be able to do so.

In throwing over traditional attitudes toward sex, the Villagers were, again, attacking simultaneously Puritanism and bourgeois morality. Their attitudes toward sex were the product of a combination of trends—the attack on Puritanism which gave the *American Mercury* its vogue, the growing equality between men and women of which the success of the suffrage movement was only one manifestation, and the "arrival" of Freud and psychoanalysis to bring sex into the center of the stage. They ranged from those engaged in a serious and genuine effort to discover a basis for a freer relationship to those for whom sex was merely a symbol and who turned to promiscuity or homosexuality to express the completeness of their defiance. The former struggled against the odds of economic and personal insecurity and the strain of city living to find a basis for personal independence. The latter used Freud to rationalize as all-important what was much nearer sheer lust than the experience with whose ramifications the psychologist dealt. In between were many who were honest in their desire to cast off the shackles of Puritanism, who might or might not lean on Freud for support, and who used the equality of the sexes as a useful concept to justify the new conduct of girls. Characteristically the latter found themselves in a conflict situation, for they had often not changed their attitudes as completely as they thought, and in spite of lip service to freedom and equality, they retained many of their bourgeois values.

The setting for all these changes was furnished, somewhat fortuitously, by Prohibition, and drink became not only an avenue of escape but a symbol of defiance. However irrelevantly, sobriety went overboard along with "virtue" and "success."

The artists as a group—painters and literary people especially—were the first to make the Village a refuge from the social controls of Main Street, and to establish the positive features of its challenge. A proper treatment of their role would call for a literary and artistic history of post-War America, for a large proportion of the writers and artists of these years resided at one time or another or had their associations in the Village. Since this is a social rather than a literary study, however, this tempting field must be passed over for a limited consideration of the social place of these artists and writers in the Village.

In the early years the stream of artists and writers who were identified with the Village included such real talent as that of Edna St. Vincent Millay or Theodore Dreiser. The fact that almost any paragraph written or spoken about the Village sounds like a textbook on modern American literature is ample testimony. These early Village residents, moreover, either originated or actively promoted pioneer efforts in such varied fields as free verse, the Little Theater movement, interior decoration, radical periodical literature. In the early days, too, this group was poor and lived impecuniously, informally, and often co-operatively. According to all testimony, many of its members constituted a fairly close group, eating together, criticizing each other's work, and, though intensely individualistic, feeling a common bond holding them together against the world.

In the post-War years, the old group of artists gradually broke up and drifted away, leaving behind them the echo of their renown and the oft-repeated question, "Is the Village still the literary capital of America? What has become of those who gave it its fame? Has the artist colony of the Village been supplied with new blood as the years have gone by?"

As the Village became better known and more generally sought as a place of residence, it lost the cheap rents which made it particularly attractive to artists and writers. At the same time, many of those who had struggled in the Village in poverty and fraternity had become famous and sufficiently prosperous to live elsewhere with greater comfort and independence. Thus, those with the money to stay could also afford to leave and those without money could not afford to remain. Some few who became successful retained their studios at high rents either because they liked the locality or because they found a Village address an asset, while some who showed little signs of achieving success found cheap quarters in out-of-the-way places and stayed on, dependent on the encouragement of others in the same position.

For those who had chosen to depart when they had had the opportunity either to go or to stay, many reasons for leaving the Village were given both by those who were left behind and by those who went. Charges that the artists had left because they had "gone bourgeois" were met with the statement that it was the Village which had gone bourgeois. The upshot of the testimony seemed to indicate that the breakup of the old artist colony had involved a gradual process of dispersion, each leaving for a personal reason when he had become bored or at odds with the group or indifferent to it. Although some moved together to places which were or became new centers, there was no group movement of artists out of the Village—no transfer of the Village to another place.

The exodus of the old group did not check the flow of new young writers and artists into the Village. These continued to come, to find themselves cheap quarters, to congregate in little groups and to struggle along with varying degrees of effectiveness and talent. It was still possible in 1930 to have the man on the next stool at a drugstore lunch counter explain that he had just come to live in the Village and was looking for "the artists" and try to sell you a portrait sketch which he had made while you were eating. A local newspaper editor, playing up the artistic side of the Village, was able to arrange with a druggist to use his window for the display of the works of Village artists, a different painter usually each week. The newcomers were both befriended and exploited by older artists, newspapermen, printers, tea-shop and speakeasy propri-

etors. Most especially they were made self-conscious, as "Village poets" or "Village painters." . . .

In contrast to the Babbitt-ridden communities from which they had escaped, virtually every group in the Village at any time was definitely art-conscious. The professional, conventional people looked upon the genuine arts with respect and discrimination, entertained a hearty contempt for the pseudos, and were quite likely to pursue some form of artistic expression themselves as an avocation. The bohemians and those whose repudiation was complete, claimed efforts toward creative expression as their *raison d'être,* quite regardless of the success of those efforts, while those who had partially discarded their traditions were more than likely to yearn toward the arts, perhaps maintaining some form of expression as an avocation, and in some cases, hoping to abandon their bread-and-butter jobs in favor of an artist's life if they should ever become sufficiently proficient to do so. The social adjustments of the artist, in their turn, varied through the whole range of Village groups, with some concentration at the more experimental end of the scale.

The group which first sought social readjustment in the Village and which numbered some of the serious artists and writers among its members was genuine in its effort to discover new values and far from wishing to abandon all parts of the code of behavior in which it had grown up. Rather, its members sought to carry forward what they regarded as vital in the American tradition and to maintain, in the face of disrupting influences, the cultural values which they had inherited. What they repudiated primarily was the money drive, the "Babbittry," the purely acquisitive values which had come to dominate the American scene. . . .

At the extreme opposite end of the scale from those professional groups who sought to perpetuate in taste their cherished social values were the out-and-out bohemians whose repudiation of the values and the controls of organized society was complete. These discarded money values to the point of making little or no provision for self-support and tossed all trace of moral earnestness and other aspects of old American culture into the scrap-heap as well. The influence of this group was out of all proportion to its actual numbers. It had come in originally, as bohemias are prone to do, in the trail of the Village's early artist colony, and had then become a distinct group in itself. In spite of the reputation which the bohemians' publicly led lives gave to the Village, not more than a small group at any one time would truly have answered to this description—would really have fallen within the category of those who deliberately disregarded the standards and the drives which governed the ordinary world, either on grounds of philosophy, preoccupation with art or laziness.

Certain houses, owned by a landlord whose reputation for befriending bohemians was known from coast to coast, housed most of these, although some were scattered in the garrets of unremodeled houses. In these apartments, no one was put out for failure to pay the rent, but was simply moved to smaller quarters or put in with another occupant. The landlord even went so far as to help out his tenants with money or food when they were badly off, or lent them typewriters. He recognized that many were shiftless and took advantage of him, that others lived from drink to drink, while others were really struggling and devoting themselves to artistic or literary pursuits. This group drifted in and out, but some members stayed on for years. The type and its habits remained constant from the earliest days of the Village until 1930, though the proportion whose artistic pretensions were real appeared to have dropped, and the homosexual types became somewhat more prominent.

The influence of the genuine bohemians extended beyond the confines of the houses where they lived and the eating-places where they met, for their reputation lured many young people who were not really bohemian in their philosophy and temperament, but eager to "see life" by living in what they considered the bohemian manner. In the course of the decade, more and more of the Village population came to consist of young single people holding ordinary jobs, coming from ordinary backgrounds. Some of these had come with the deliberate intent of following the bohemian path. Many had come to live in the Village simply because it was convenient or offered the right type of apartment, but even these found themselves exposed to the contagion of bohemianism. Other people who did not live in the Village, but resided with their families in other parts of the metropolitan area, were also drawn there for social life. The hangouts which went in most heavily for "bohemian atmosphere" were centers for people from Brooklyn or the Bronx.

The pseudo-bohemians developed two closely related social institutions, the hangout and the studio party. Since their daytime occupations were the minimum compromise with economic necessity, their night activities were the focus of their life. Formal societies constituted to them part of the pattern which they repudiated. At the same time their insecurity and the directions of their escape produced a gregariousness of habit which led them to gather nightly in some studio apartment or public meeting place. To capitalize this gregariousness, a succession of gathering places were opened, some serving sandwiches and furnishing informal entertainment, others, more imposing in name but not in practice, calling themselves studio salons or clubs. They offered unlimited opportunities for contacts to those who sought to join this type of group. A description of one of these hangouts in 1930 would have been equally applicable to its series of predecessors.

"Jo's" was located in the basement of a tenement building. In the low, narrow room, cheap, brightly colored tables, rickety chairs, a few booths and an old piano were crowded as tight as they could be jammed. Liquor was not served, but it was assumed that the patrons would bring it, and order sandwiches and ginger ale. The place was usually crowded and always informal. Girls making a first visit to the place could be sure that the men beside whom they found themselves seated would assume that they were a party for the evening and night. If the girls were first at a table, they were sure to be joined. From time to time someone started to play the piano and people danced in the crowded aisles between the tables with whatever strangers they happened to be sitting beside. The proprietor stood by the door, greeting everybody, eyeing all newcomers and making announcements. Many of those present were young girls and boys with pale faces and circled eyes who drank heavily. The rest were a few middle-aged men who had obviously come for relaxation and to pick up a girl, and a number of older people, some with an artistic or literary past, who were known as habitués. A young Chinese communist came to pick up someone who could help him translate and criticize his work. Certain familiar figures who were always known to be trying to borrow money were cold-shouldered by everyone. A couple of young girls from the South who obviously came from substantial homes and a cultivated background, were regularly present and conspicuous, dancing together and constantly drunk.

These people had two preoccupations — sex and drink. In the early years of the decade, free love and promiscuity had been a sufficient subject for talk and entertainment in most groups. By 1930, promiscuity was tame and homosexuality had become the expected thing. One girl who came nightly was the joke of the place because she was trying so hard to be a Lesbian, but when she got drunk she forgot and let the men dance with her. A favorite entertainer was a "pansy" whose best stunt was a take-off on being a "pansy." To lend a touch of intellectuality and to give people a sense of activity, the proprietor set aside two nights each week for discussion or performance by regular patrons. These evenings, however, did not interrupt the group's major preoccupation, for the subjects chosen for discussion were such things as "the social position of a gigolo" and "what is sex appeal?" On the latter subject, the views of the Lesbians present were especially called for.

Studio parties followed the style of Jo's with only slightly greater privacy, while the clubs and salons were distinguished only by the fact that they charged admission, more regularly had a program, and laid somewhat less stress upon drink. Their literary and artistic pretensions resembled Jo's "intellectual" evenings, with the subjects for lectures and discussions also featuring sex. The "poetry" which was read or hung about the walls was in a similar vein. Their clientèle varied more widely and contained a larger proportion who lived elsewhere in the city and who sought rather to gain an evening's excitement in the midst of a more or less conventional life than to abandon such a life altogether.

For this group sex in its most irresponsible form was a means of escape either from the type of life in which they had grown up or from some inadequacy in themselves. In the absence of clinical data, it was not possible to determine how many of the group were running away from personality problems and family situations and how many from the emptiness of inherited social codes. Neither was it possible to determine the extent to which repudiation was a mere episode or a permanent attitude. A little fragmentary and inconclusive evidence suggested that, for a substantial number, this type of escape was more than a temporary phase. For those who lived elsewhere in the city and simply came down for their entertainment, it may well have had little permanent importance. But for those who came from a distance to live in the Village, a more serious break may well have been involved. The testimony of the doctor whose office was located most conveniently to the center of such activity bore vigorous witness to the number of girls whose health was permanently impaired. For individuals who for any long period of time remained part of this group, the possibility of returning to the home communities, once they had so thoroughly repudiated the values of these communities, was certainly reduced. The older persons who had become long-time habitués testified by their persons to this potentiality. On the other hand, the proprietor of one of the less extreme of the hangouts reported many former patrons who had settled down to bourgeois lives.

Of all the groups in the Village, this one had the widest influence on the rest of the country, for it helped to popularize the "wild party" from one end of the land to the other; it was the purely negative set of values which this group developed that set its stamp upon America during these years. "It's well to remember that the Village isn't unique," observed one of the interviewers who was working on this study. "If that necking party I went to in Brooklyn last night had been in the Village, I'd have taken it for 'typical'— but there it was, as wild as you please, and right in the most substantial part of respectable Brooklyn." . . .

Thus the Villagers, virtually without social institutions, scornful of bourgeois values, seeking escape through sex, rationalizing their conduct with the aid of Freud and of art, and in despair of social reconstruction, developed an individualism as irresponsible and as extreme as that of the local Italians who were out for themselves. Through their actions, they made the Village a symbol of defiance to whatever the established social order might be. It mattered little that most who lived in the Village did not share in the extremer forms of its reputation or that the rest of the country adopted many of the habits which had been unique in the Village at an earlier time. Greenwich Village remained always the place where one could go farther than in other communities, and as such it acted as a social leaven for the rest of the country. Its manners and attitudes, its art forms and its gin parties, became familiar from coast to coast. Herein lay its entirely uncalculable social influence, an influence which grew as it drew less exceptional and adventurous residents than it had in its early days.

But in its own social life the Village offered no solution to the cultural problems which drove people to the area. Escape it offered but not solution. It accelerated the breaking of old forms, but it contributed no new ones to take their place. In the face of cultural disintegration, it either fostered escape or erected the individual as a psychological entity into an end in himself.

JOHN W. WARD (b. 1922) was granted a Ph.D.
in American Civilization from the University of
Minnesota. He has taught at Princeton University
and Amherst College and is currently president
of Amherst College. Ward has been a Guggenheim
fellow and a Fulbright lecturer and is the author
of *Andrew Jackson, Symbol of an Age* (1955). His
article "The Meaning of Lindbergh's Flight" was
first published in the *American Quarterly* (1958)
and is a discerning analysis of an event that
became more significant in symbol than reality.
How does Lindbergh's flight manifest the
frustrations of the Twenties? Why did Americans
take the aviator as their special hero? Why were
sports figures and movie stars idolized in these
years as never before?*

John W. Ward

Lindbergh: Linking the Future to the Past

On Friday, May 20, 1927, at 7:52 A.M., Charles A. Lindbergh took off in a silver-winged monoplane and flew from the United States to France. With this flight Lindbergh became the first man to fly alone across the Atlantic Ocean. The log of flight 33 of "The Spirit of St. Louis" reads: "Roosevelt Field, Long Island, New York, to Le Bourget Aerodrome, Paris, France. 33 hrs. 30 min." Thus was the fact of Lindbergh's achievement easily put down. But the meaning of Lindbergh's flight lay hidden in the next sentence of the log: "(Fuselage fabric badly torn by souvenir hunters.)"

When Lindbergh landed at Le Bourget he is supposed to have said, "Well, we've done it." A contemporary writer asked "Did what?" Lindbergh "had no idea of what he had done. He thought he had simply flown from New York to Paris. What he had really done was something far greater. He had fired the imagination of mankind." From the moment of Lindbergh's flight people recognized that something more was involved than the mere fact of the physical leap from New York to Paris. "Lindbergh," wrote John Erskine, "served as a metaphor." But what the metaphor stood for was not easy to say. The *New York Times* remarked then that "there has been no complete and satisfactory explanation of the enthusiasm and acclaim for Captain Lind-

---

*John W. Ward, "The Meaning of Lindbergh's Flight," *American Quarterly,* X (Spring, 1958), pp. 3–16. Copyright, 1968, Trustees of the University of Pennsylvania. Reprinted by permission.

bergh." Looking back on the celebration of Lindbergh, one can see now that the American people were trying to understand Lindbergh's flight, to grasp its meaning, and through it, perhaps, to grasp the meaning of their own experience. Was the flight the achievement of a heroic, solitary, unaided individual? Or did the flight represent the triumph of the machine, the success of an industrially organized society? These questions were central to the meaning of Lindbergh's flight. They were also central to the lives of the people who made Lindbergh their hero.

The flight demanded attention in its own right, of course, quite apart from whatever significance it might have. Lindbergh's story had all the makings of great drama. Since 1919 there had been a standing prize of $25,000 to be awarded to the first aviator who could cross the Atlantic in either direction between the United States and France in a heavier-than-air craft. In the spring of 1927 there promised to be what the *New York Times* called "the most spectacular race ever held — 3,600 miles over the open sea to Paris." The scene was dominated by veteran pilots. On the European side were the French aces, Nungesser and Coli; on the American side, Commander Richard E. Byrd, in a big tri-motored Fokker monoplane, led a group of contestants. Besides Byrd, who had already flown over the North Pole, there were Commander Davis, flying a ship named in honor of the American Legion which had put up $100,000 to finance his attempt, Clarence Chamberlin, who had already set a world's endurance record of more than fifty-one hours in the air in a Bellanca tri-motored plane, and Captain René Fonck, the French war ace, who had come to America to fly a Sikorsky aircraft.

The hero was unheard of and unknown. He was on the West Coast supervising the construction of a single-engined plane to cost only ten thousand dollars.

Then fate played its part. It seemed impossible that Lindbergh could get his plane built and east to New York in time to challenge his better equipped and more famous rivals. But in quick succession a series of disasters cleared his path. On April 16, Commander Byrd's "America" crashed on its test flight, crushing the leg of Floyd Bennett who was one of the crew and injuring Byrd's hand and wrist. On April 24, Clarence Chamberlin cracked up in his Bellanca, not seriously, but enough to delay his plans. Then on April 26, Commander Davis and his co-pilot lost their lives as the "American Legion" crashed on its final test flight. In ten days, accidents had stopped all of Lindbergh's American rivals. Nungesser and Coli, however, took off in their romantically named ship, "The White Bird," from Le Bourget on May 8. The world waited and Lindbergh, still on the West Coast, decided to try to fly the Pacific. But Nungesser and Coli were never seen again. As rumors filled the newspapers, as reports came in that the "White Bird" was seen over Newfoundland, over Boston, over the Atlantic, it soon became apparent that Nungesser and Coli had failed, dropping to their death in some unknown grave. Disaster had touched every ship entered in the trans-Atlantic race.

Now, with the stage cleared, Lindbergh entered. He swooped across the continent in two great strides, landing only in St. Louis. The first leg of his flight established a new distance record but all eyes were on the Atlantic and the feat received little notice. Curiously, the first time Lindbergh appeared in the headlines of the New York papers was Friday, the thirteenth. By this time Byrd and Chamberlin were ready once again but the weather had closed in and kept all planes on the ground. Then, after a week of fretful waiting, on the night of May 19, on the way into New York to see "Rio Rita," Lindbergh received a report that the weather was breaking over the ocean. He hurried back to Roosevelt Field to haul his plane out onto a wet, dripping runway. After mechanics painfully loaded the plane's gas by hand, the wind shifted, as fate played its last trick. A muddy runway and an adverse wind. Whatever the elements, whatever the fates, the decisive act is the hero's, and Lindbergh made his choice. Providing a chorus to the action, the *Herald Tribune* reported that Lindbergh lifted the overloaded plane into the sky "by his indomitable will alone."

The parabola of the action was as clean as the arc of Lindbergh's flight. The drama should have ended with the landing of "The Spirit of St. Louis" at Le Bourget. That is where Lindbergh wanted it to end. In *"WE,"* written immediately after the flight, and in *The Spirit of St. Louis,* written twenty-six years later, Lindbergh chose to end his accounts there. But the flight turned out to be only the first act in the part Lindbergh was to play.

Lindbergh was so innocent of his future that on his flight he carried letters of introduction. The hysterical response, first of the French and then of his own countrymen, had been no part of his careful plans. In *"WE,"* after Lindbergh's narrative of the flight, the publisher wrote: "When Lindbergh came to tell the story of his welcome at Paris, London, Brussels, Washington, New York, and St. Louis he found himself up against a tougher problem than flying the Atlantic." So another writer completed

the account in the third person. He suggested that "the reason Lindbergh's story is different is that when his plane came to a halt on Le Bourget field that black night in Paris, Lindbergh the man kept on going. The phenomenon of Lindbergh took its start with his flight across the ocean; but in its entirety it was almost as distinct from that flight as though he had never flown at all."

Lindbergh's private life ended with his flight to Paris. The drama was no longer his, it was the public's. "The outburst of unanimous acclaim was at once personal and symbolic," said the *American Review of Reviews.* From the moment of success there were two Lindberghs, the private Lindbergh and the public Lindbergh. The latter was the construction of the imagination of Lindbergh's time, fastened on to an unwilling person. The tragedy of Lindbergh's career is that he could never accept the role assigned him. He always believed he might keep his two lives separate. But from the moment he landed at Le Bourget, Lindbergh became, as the *New Republic* noted, *"ours . . . .* He is no longer permitted to be himself. He is US personified. He is the United States." Ambassador Herrick introduced Lindbergh to the French, saying, "This young man from out of the West brings you better than anything else the spirit of America," and wired to President Coolidge, "Had we searched all America we could not have found a better type than young Lindbergh to represent the spirit and high purpose of our people." This was Lindbergh's fate, to be a type. A writer in the *North American Review* felt that Lindbergh represented "the dominant American character," he "images the best" about the United States. And an ecstatic female in the *American Magazine,* who began by saying that Lindbergh "is a sort of symbol. . . . He is the dream that is in our hearts," concluded that the American public responded so wildly to Lindbergh because of "the thrill of possessing, in him, our dream of what *we* really and truly want to be." The act of possession was so complete that articles since have attempted to discover the "real" Lindbergh, that enigmatic and taciturn figure behind the public mask. But it is no less difficult to discern the features of the public Lindbergh, that symbolic figure who presented to the imagination of his time all the yearnings and buried desires of its dream for itself.

Lindbergh's flight came at the end of a decade marked by social and political corruption and by a sense of moral loss. The heady idealism of the First World War had been succeeded by a deep cynicism as to the war's real purpose. The naïve belief that virtue could be legislated was violated by the vast discrepancy between the law and the social habits of prohibition. A philosophy of relativism had become the uneasy rationale of a nation which had formerly believed in moral absolutes. The newspapers agreed that Lindbergh's chief worth was his spiritual and moral value. His story was held to be "in striking contrast with the sordid unhallowed themes that have for months steeped the imaginations and thinking of the people." Or, as another had it, "there is good reason why people should hail Lindbergh and give him honor. He stands out in a grubby world as an inspiration."

Lindbergh gave the American people a glimpse of what they liked to think themselves to be at a time when they feared they had deserted their own vision of themselves. The grubbiness of the twenties had a good deal to do with the shining quality of Lindbergh's success, especially when one remembers that

Lindbergh's flight was not as unexampled as our national memory would have it. The Atlantic was not unconquered when Lindbergh flew. A British dirigible had twice crossed the Atlantic before 1919 and on May 8 of that year three naval seaplanes left Rockaway, New York, and one, the NC–4 manned by a crew of five, got through to Plymouth, England. A month later, Captain John Alcock, an Englishman, with Arthur W. Browne, an American, flew the first heavier-than-air land plane across the Atlantic nonstop, from Newfoundland to Ireland, to win twice the money Lindbergh did, a prize of $50,000 offered by the London *Daily Mail.* Alcock's and Browne's misfortune was to land in a soft and somnolent Irish peat bog instead of before the cheering thousands of London or Paris. Or perhaps they should have flown in 1927.

The wild medley of public acclaim and the homeric strivings of editors make one realize that the response to Lindbergh involved a mass ritual in which America celebrated itself more than it celebrated Lindbergh. Lindbergh's flight was the occasion of a public act of regeneration in which the nation momentarily rededicated itself to something, the loss of which was keenly felt. It was said again and again that "Lindy" taught America "to lift its eyes up to Heaven." Heywood Broun, in his column in the *New York World,* wrote that this "tall young man raised up and let us see the potentialities of the human spirit." Broun felt that the flight proved that, though "we are small and fragile," it "isn't true that there is no health in us." Lindbergh's flight provided the moment, but the meaning of the flight is to be found in the deep and pervasive need for renewal which the flight brought to the surface of public feeling. When Lindbergh appeared at the nation's capital, the *Washington Post* observed,

"He was given that frenzied acclaim which comes from the depths of the people." In New York, where 4,000,000 people saw him, a reporter wrote that the dense and vociferous crowds were swept, as Lindbergh passed, "with an emotion tense and inflammable." The *Literary Digest* suggested that the answer to the hero-worship of Lindbergh would "throw an interesting light on the psychology of our times and of the American people."

The *Nation* noted about Lindbergh that "there was something lyric as well as heroic about the apparition of this young Lochinvar who suddenly came out of the West and who flew all unarmed and all alone. It is the kind of stuff which the ancient Greeks would have worked into a myth and the medieval Scots into a border ballad. . . . But what we have in the case of Lindbergh is an actual, an heroic and an exhaustively exposed experience which exists by suggestion in the form of poetry." The *Nation* quickly qualified its statement by observing that reporters were as far as possible from being poets and concluded that the discrepancy between the fact and the celebration of it was not poetry, perhaps, but "magic on a vast scale." Yet the *Nation* might have clung to its insight that the public meaning of Lindbergh's flight was somehow poetic. The vast publicity about Lindbergh corresponds in one vital particular with the poetic vision. Poetry, said William Butler Yeats, contains opposites; so did Lindbergh. Lindbergh did not mean one thing, he meant many things. The image of itself which America contemplated in the public person of Lindbergh was full of conflict; it was, in a word, dramatic.

To heighten the drama, Lindbergh did it alone. He was the "lone eagle" and a full exploration of that fact takes one deep into the emotional meaning of his success. Not only the *Nation* found Sir Walter Scott's lines on Lochinvar appropriate: "he rode all unarmed and he rode all alone." Newspapers and magazines were deluged with amateur poems that vindicated one rhymester's wry comment, "Go conquer the perils / That lurk in the skies - - / And you'll get bum poems / Right up to your eyes." The *New York Times,* that alone received more than two hundred poems, observed in trying to summarize the poetic deluge that "the fact that he flew alone made the strongest impression." Another favorite tribute was Kipling's "The Winners," with its refrain, "He travels the fastest who travels alone." The others who had conquered the Atlantic and those like Byrd and Chamberlin who were trying at the same time were not traveling alone and they hardly rode unarmed. Other than Lindbergh, all the contestants in the trans-Atlantic race had unlimited backing, access to the best planes, and all were working in teams, carrying at least one co-pilot to share the long burden of flying the plane. So a writer in the New York *Sun,* in a poem called "The Flying Fool," a nickname that Lindbergh despised, celebrated Lindbergh's flight: ". . . no kingly plane for him; / No endless data, comrades, moneyed chums; / No boards, no councils, no directors grim— / He plans ALONE . . . and takes luck as it comes."

Upon second thought, it must seem strange that the long distance flight of an airplane, the achievement of a highly advanced and organized technology, should be the occasion for hymns of praise to the solitary unaided man. Yet the National Geographic Society, when it presented a medal to Lindbergh, wrote on the presentation scroll, "Courage, when it goes alone, has ever caught men's imaginations," and compared Lindbergh to Robinson Crusoe and the trailmakers in our own West. But Lindbergh and Robinson Crusoe, the one in his helmet and fur-lined flying coat and the other in his wild goatskins, do not easily co-exist. Even if Robinson Crusoe did have a tidy capital investment in the form of a well-stocked shipwreck, he still did not have a ten thousand dollar machine under him.

Lindbergh, in nearly every remark about his flight and in his own writings about it, resisted the tendency to exploit the flight as the achievement of an individual. He never said "I," he always said "We." The plane was not to go unrecognized. Nevertheless, there persisted a tendency to seize upon the flight as a way of celebrating the self-sufficient individual, so that among many others an Ohio newspaper could describe Lindbergh as this "self-contained, self-reliant, courageous young man [who] ranks among the great pioneers of history." The strategy here was a common one, to make Lindbergh a "pioneer" and thus to link him with a long and vital tradition of individualism in the American experience. Colonel Theodore Roosevelt, himself the son of a famous exponent of self-reliance, said to reporters at his home in Oyster Bay that "Captain Lindbergh personifies the daring of youth. Daniel Boone, David Crocket [*sic*], and men of that type played a lone hand and made America. Lindbergh is their lineal descendant." In *Outlook* magazine, immediately below an enthusiastic endorsement of Lindbergh's own remarks on the importance of his machine and his scientific instruments, there was the statement, "Charles Lindbergh is the heir of all that we like to think is best in America. He is of the stuff out of which have been made the pioneers that opened up the wilderness, first on the Atlantic coast, and then

in our great West. His are the qualities which we, as a people, must nourish." It is in this mood that one suspects it was important that Lindbergh came out of the West and rode all alone.

Another common metaphor in the attempt to place Lindbergh's exploit was to say that he had opened a new "frontier." To speak of the air as a "frontier" was to invoke an interpretation of the meaning of American history which had sources deep in American experience, but the frontier of the airplane is hardly the frontier of the trailmakers of the old West. Rather than an escape into the self-sufficient simplicity of the American past, the machine which made Lindbergh's flight possible represented an advance into a complex industrial present. The difficulty lay in using an instance of modern life to celebrate the virtues of the past, to use an extreme development of an urban industrial society to insist upon the significance of the frontier in American life.

A little more than a month after Lindbergh's flight, Joseph K. Hart in *Survey* magazine reached back to Walt Whitman's poem for the title of an article on Lindbergh: "O Pioneer." A school had made Lindbergh an honorary alumnus but Hart protested there was little available evidence "that he was educated in *schools.*" "We must look elsewhere for our explanation," Hart wrote and he looked to the experience of Lindbergh's youth when "everything that he ever did . . . he did by himself. He lived more to himself than most boys." And, of course, Lindbergh lived to himself in the only place conceivably possible, in the world of nature, on a Minnesota farm. "There he developed in the companionship of woods and fields, animals and machines, his audaciously natural and simple personality." The word, "machines," jars as it intrudes into Hart's idyllic pastoral landscape and betrays Hart's difficulty in relating the setting of nature upon which he wishes to insist with the fact that its product spent his whole life tinkering with machines, from motorcycles to airplanes. But except for that one word, Hart proceeds in uncritical nostalgia to show that "a lone trip across the Atlantic was not impossible for a boy who had grown up in the solitude of the woods and waters." If Lindbergh was "clear-headed, naif, untrained in the ways of cities," it was because he had "that 'natural simplicity' which Fenimore Cooper used to attribute to the pioneer hero of his Leatherstocking Tales." Hart rejected the notion that any student "bent to all the conformities" of formal training could have done what Lindbergh did. "Must we not admit," he asked, "that this pioneering urge remained to this audacious youth because he had never submitted completely to the repressions of the world and its jealous institutions?"

Only those who insist on reason will find it strange that Hart should use the industrial achievement of the airplane to reject the urban, institutionalized world of industrialism. Hart was dealing with something other than reason; he was dealing with the emotion evoked by Lindbergh's solitude. He recognized that people wished to call Lindbergh a "genius" because that "would release him from the ordinary rules of existence." That way, "we could rejoice with him in his triumph, and then go back to the contracted routines of our institutional ways [because] ninety-nine percent of us must be content to be shaped and moulded by the routine ways and forms of the world to the routine tasks of life." It is in the word, "must," that the pathos of this interpretation of the phenomenon of Lindbergh lies. The world had changed

from the open society of the pioneer to the close-knit, interdependent world of a modern machine-oriented civilization. The institutions of a highly corporate industrial society existed as a constant reproach to a people who liked to believe that the meaning of its experience was embodied in the formless, independent life of the frontier. Like Thomas Jefferson who identified American virtue with nature and saw the city as a "great sore" on the public body, Hart concluded that "certainly, in the response that the world— especially the world of great cities—has made to the performance of this midwestern boy, we can read of the homesickness of the human soul, immured in city canyons and routine tasks, for the freer world of youth, for the open spaces of the pioneer, for the joy of battling with nature and clean storms once more on the frontiers of the earth."

The social actuality which made the adulation of Lindbergh possible had its own irony for the notion that America's strength lay in its simple uncomplicated beginnings. For the public response to Lindbergh to have reached the proportions it did, the world had by necessity to be the intricately developed world of modern mass communications. But more than irony was involved. Ultimately, the emotion attached to Lindbergh's flight involved no less than a whole theory about American history. By singling out the fact that Lindbergh rode alone, and by naming him a pioneer of the frontier, the public projected its sense that the source of America's strength lay somewhere in the past and that Lindbergh somehow meant that America must look backward in time to rediscover some lost virtue. The mood was nostalgic and American history was read as a decline, a decline measured in terms of America's advance into an urban, institutionalized way of life which made solitary achievement increasingly beyond the reach of ninety-nine per cent of the people. Because Lindbergh's ancestors were Norse, it was easy to call him a "Viking" and extend the emotion far into the past when all frontiers were open. He became the "Columbus" of another new world to conquer as well as the "Lochinvar" who rode all alone. But there was always the brute, irreducible fact that Lindbergh's exploit was a victory of the machine over the barriers of nature. If the only response to Lindbergh had been a retreat to the past, we would be involved with a mass cultural neurosis, the inability of America to accept reality, the reality of the world in which it lived. But there was another aspect, one in which the public celebrated the machine and the highly organized society of which it was a product. The response to Lindbergh reveals that the American people were deeply torn between conflicting interpretations of their own experience. By calling Lindbergh a pioneer, the people could read into American history the necessity of turning back to the frontier past. Yet the people could also read American history in terms of progress into the industrial future. They could do this by emphasizing the machine which was involved in Lindbergh's flight.

Lindbergh came back from Europe in an American man-of-war, the cruiser *Memphis.* It seems he had contemplated flying on, around the whole world perhaps, but less adventurous heads prevailed and dictated a surer mode of travel for so valuable a piece of public property. The *New Republic* protested against bringing America's hero of romance home in a warship. If he had returned on a great liner, that would have been one thing. "One's first trip on an ocean-liner is a great adventure—the novelty of it, the many people of all kinds and conditions, floating for a week in a tiny compact world of their own." But to return on the *Memphis,* "to be put on a gray battleship with a collection of people all of the same stripe, in a kind of ship that has as much relation to the life of the sea as a Ford factory has! We might as well have put him in a pneumatic tube and shot him across the Atlantic." The interesting thing about the *New Republic's* protest against the unromantic, regimented life of a battleship is that the image it found appropriate was the Ford assembly line. It was this reaction against the discipline of a mechanized society that probably led to the nostalgic image of Lindbergh as a remnant of a past when romance was possible for the individual, when life held novelty and society was variegated rather than uniform. But what the Ford Assembly Line represents, a society committed to the path of full mechanization, was what lay behind Lindbergh's romantic success. A long piece in the Sunday *New York Times,* "Lindbergh Symbolizes the Genius of America," reminded its readers of the too obvious fact that "without an airplane he could not have flown at all." Lindbergh "is, indeed, the Icarus of the twentieth century; not himself an inventor of his own wings, but a son of that omnipotent Daedalus whose ingenuity has created the modern world." The point was that modern America was the creation of modern industry. Lindbergh "reveres his 'ship' as a noble expression of mechanical wisdom. . . . Yet in this reverence . . . Lindbergh is not an exception. What he means by the Spirit of St. Louis is really the spirit of America. The mechanical genius, which is discerned in Henry Ford as well as in Charles A. Lindbergh, is in the very atmosphere of [the] country." In contrast to a sentiment that feared the enforced discipline of the machine there existed an attitude of reverence for its power.

Lindbergh led the way in the celebration of the machine, not only implicitly by including his plane when he said "we," but by direct statement. In Paris he told newspapermen, "You fellows have not said enough about that wonderful motor." Rarely have two more taciturn figures confronted one another than when Lindbergh returned to Washington and Calvin Coolidge pinned the Distinguished Flying Cross on him, but in his brief remarks Coolidge found room to express his particular delight that Lindbergh should have given equal credit to the airplane. "For we are proud," said the President, "that in every particular this silent partner represented American genius and industry. I am told that more than 100 separate companies furnished materials, parts or service in its construction."

The flight was not the heroic lone success of a single daring individual, but the climax of the co-operative effort of an elaborately interlocked technology. The day after Coolidge's speech, Lindbergh said at another ceremony in Washington that the honor should "not go to the pilot alone but to American science and genius which had given years of study to the advancement of aeronautics." "Some things," he said, "should be taken into due consideration in connection with our flight that have not heretofore been given due weight. That is just what made this flight possible. It was not the act of a single pilot. It was the culmination of twenty years of aeronautical research and the assembling together of all that was practicable and best in American aviation." The flight, concluded Lindbergh, "represented American industry."

The worship of the machine which was embodied in the public's response to Lindbergh exalted those very aspects which were denigrated in the celebration of the flight as the work of a heroic individual. Organization and careful method were what lay behind the flight, not individual self-sufficiency and daring romance. One magazine hailed the flight as a "triumph of mechanical engineering." "It is not to be forgotten that this era is the work not so much of brave aviators as of engineers, who have through patient and protracted effort been steadily improving the construction of airplanes." The lesson to be learned from Lindbergh's flight, thought a writer in the *Independent,* "is that the splendid human and material aspects of America need to be organized for the ordinary, matter of fact service of society." The machine meant organization, the careful rationalization of activity of a Ford assembly line, it meant planning, and, if it meant the loss of spontaneous individual action, it meant the material betterment of society. Lindbergh meant not a retreat to the free life of the frontier past but an emergence into the time when "the machine began to take first place in the public mind—the machine and the organization that made its operation possible on a large scale." A poet on this side of the matter wrote, "All day I felt the pull / Of the steel miracle." The machine was not a devilish engine which would enthrall mankind, it was the instrument which would lead to a new paradise. But the direction of history implicit in the machine was toward the future, not the past; the meaning of history was progress, not decline, and America should not lose faith in the future betterment of society. An address by a Harvard professor, picked up by the *Magazine of Business,* made all this explicit. "We commonly take Social Progress for granted," said Edwin F. Gay, "but the doctrine of Social Progress is one of the great revolutionary ideas which have powerfully affected our modern world." There was a danger, however, that the idea "may be in danger of becoming a commonplace or a butt of criticism." The speaker recognized why this might be. America was "worn and disillusioned after the Great War." Logically, contentment should have gone with so optimistic a creed, yet the American people were losing faith. So Lindbergh filled an emotional need even where a need should have been lacking. "He has come like a shining vision to revive the hope of mankind." The high ideals of faith in progress "had almost come to seem like hollow words to us—but now here he is, emblematic of heroes yet to inhabit this world. Our belief in Social Progress is justified symbolically in him."

It is a long flight from New York to Paris; it is a still longer flight from the fact of Lindbergh's achievement to the burden imposed upon it by the imagination of his time. But it is in that further flight that lies the full meaning of Lindbergh. His role was finally a double one. His flight provided an opportunity for the people to project their own emotions into his act and their emotions involved finally two attitudes toward the meaning of their own experience. One view had it that America represented a brief escape from the course of history, an emergence into a new and open world with the self-sufficient individual at its center. The other said that America represented a stage in historical evolution and that its fulfillment lay in the development of society. For one, the meaning of America lay in the past; for the other in the future. For one, the American ideal was an escape from institutions, from the forms of society, and from limitations put upon the free individual; for the other, the American ideal was the elaboration of the com-

plex institutions which made modern society possible, an acceptance of the discipline of the machine, and the achievement of the individual within a context of which he was only a part. The two views were contradictory but both were possible and both were present in the public's reaction to Lindbergh's flight.

The Sunday newspapers announced that Lindbergh had reached Paris and in the very issue whose front pages were covered with Lindbergh's story the magazine section of the *New York Times* featured an article by the British philosopher, Bertrand Russell. The magazine had, of course, been made up too far in advance to take advantage of the news about Lindbergh. Yet, in a prophetic way, Russell's article was about Lindbergh. Russell hailed the rise to power of the United States because he felt that in the "new life that is America's" in the twentieth century "the new outlook appropriate to machinery [would] become more completely dominant than in the old world." Russell sensed that some might be unwilling to accept the machine, but "whether we like this new outlook or not," he wrote, "is of little importance." Why one might not was obvious. A society built on the machine, said Russell, meant "the diminution in the value and independence of the individual. Great enterprises tend more and more to be collective, and in an industrialized world the interference of the community with the individual must be more intense." Russell realized that while the co-operative effort involved in machine technology makes man collectively more lordly, it makes the individual more submissive. "I do not see how it is to be avoided," he concluded.

People are not philosophers. They did not see how the conflict between a machine society and the free individual was to be avoided either. But neither were they ready to accept the philosopher's statement of the problem. In Lindbergh, the people celebrated both the self-sufficient individual and the machine. Americans still celebrate both. . . .

A distinguished psychiatrist, FRANZ ALEXANDER (1891–1964) was born in Budapest, Hungary, where he received the doctor of medicine degree in 1913. After postgraduate work at the Psychiatric Hospital of the University of Berlin, Dr. Alexander came to the United States in 1930, becoming a naturalized citizen eight years later. From 1938–1956 he was professor of psychiatry at the University of Illinois, and later was clinical professor of psychology at the University of Southern California and director of the Psychiatric and Psychosomatic Research Institute at Mt. Sinai Hospital in Los Angeles. In addition to his penetrating *Our Age of Unreason* (1942), he is the author of *Fundamentals of Psychoanalysis* (1948), *Psychosomatic Medicine* (1950), and *The Western Mind in Transition* (1960).*

Franz Alexander

Frontier Individualism in a Corporate Society

At the present time we are witnessing the transition from oligarchy into a constitutional but more centralized government. What we are interested in here is primarily the magnitude of the cultural lag resulting from this profound change in social structure from frontier individualism into a consolidated civilization.

. . . There are two sensitive indicators of the cultural lag—crime and mental disturbances. The American criminal does not accept the fact that the days of unlimited individualism are over, and becomes the Quixotic defender of anarchistic individualism.

The profound distrust of law goes back to the colonial days. The laws passed in Parliament were not always wise or adjusted to the needs of the New World. Thus, the "colonists got in the habit of deciding themselves as individuals which laws they would observe and which they would ignore or even forcibly resist". . . . Later, the Frontiersmen assumed the same attitude toward the law-enforcing tendencies of the East as the colonists had toward the mother country. The American criminal of our day represents a deterioration and caricature of this individualistic spirit of the past. The economic factors in this type of criminality are negligible in comparison with the ideological.

The study of criminal personalities has revealed that apart from rational

*From Franz Alexander, *Our Age of Unreason* (Philadelphia: J. B. Lippincott Company, 1942), pp. 300–312. Reprinted without footnotes by permission of Anita V. Alexander.

motives like the desire for gain, other more powerful emotional factors drive individuals to crime. An excessive desire for prestige, the wish to appear daring and independent—a "tough guy"—has been found frequently as such an emotional factor, especially in the young. . . . The reason for this is probably to be found in the cultural history of the country. The ideal of the successful, resourceful, brave, self-made man who owes everything to himself and nothing to anybody else is the traditional ideal. It is obvious that these virtues were extremely important in the Frontier days and overshadowed any others in the conquest of a vast continent and in the rapid development of a new civilization.

In a remarkably short period, however, the conditions of the Frontier have changed to those of an organized and standardized industrial structure. We have recognized that spiritual tradition changes more slowly than the social structure and that this constitutes a major obstacle in the adjustment to the existing social conditions. The great majority of young men are still reared with ideals of individual initiative, endurance, self-reliance, and courage like their pioneer forefathers, but when they grow up they are exposed to a world in which opportunities for individual initiative, bravado, and individual accomplishment are extremely limited. Most of them must become employees in a big industrial plant or some other organization which offers little play for those pioneer virtues which they learned early to admire. Instead of initiative, a mechanical standardized performance is required; instead of an enterprising and adventurous spirit, rigid subordination to a trade union is demanded. In an expanding civilization the individual can expect success as a result of endurance and personal accomplishments but in an over-organized industrial civilization in which unemployment recurs periodically, the economic cycle, not personal efficiency, determines success or failure in finding employment and keeping it. The old ideals are alive but their realization becomes daily more difficult. One escape from this dilemma is criminality and the logic of the emotions explains why this solution is appealing. In the hierarchy of values independence and success stand highest. Everything else, even respect for the law, comes second. Driven by an inner need to be successful through personal initiative, the individual resorts to a pathological form of individualism and adventure,—crime. An existence regulated by monotonous routine, so common today, is diametrically opposed to the Frontier tradition and this explains the appeal of those films in which the life of today is depicted as offering unlimited possibilities. The crowds admire the hero, the young inventor or the newspaper man who reaches the top at one stride and seize eagerly upon these fantastic substitutes for real life. The secret of this appeal is a kind of anachronism, for the films adapt the materials of contemporary life to their deceptive revival of past conditions. Without this fantastic substitute, discontent with present conditions would be even more unbearable for the majority of people.

Let us, however, return to the problem of crime. The emotional tensions which I have described are common today, yet only a few choose to solve the differences between their ambitions and the possibilities of their fulfillment by breaking the law. There must be a reason why this tension becomes so excessive in some that they overcome the fear of punishment under its pressure and take the risk of jail in order to follow the drive for success by independent, dangerous, and courageous acts.

Our investigation of this question has led me to a peculiar and paradoxical conclusion. I have found the desire—I would prefer to say compulsion—to achieve success by aggressiveness and toughness, by individual accomplishment without the aid of others, strongest in those who unconsciously crave dependence. This powerful, repressed wish for dependence is rejected by the conscious portion of the personality, which because of its social training values independence and individualism as the highest virtues. In order to deny the secret dependent tendencies which are felt by the rest of the personality as signs of weakness and effeminacy, there is an excessive tendency in the opposite direction, toward aggressiveness, a kind of exaggerated masculinity. This attitude constitutes a phobia of being considered a sissy and everything which faintly suggests dependence, help, subordination even to the social order, the prescriptions of the law, are felt to be signs of effeminacy. This explains the peculiar phenomenon that those individuals in which this emotional situation is especially strongly developed look upon every "Public Enemy Number 1" as a hero.

It should be emphasized that in psychology it is extremely important to pay attention to quantities. The emotional situation which I have described is characteristic not only of America but of all western civilization which has been based on competition. To a certain extent a high regard for personal accomplishment and independence is common to the entire Western World. The pioneer history of this country explains why this attitude is more pronounced here than elsewhere and why a secret admiration of the coura-

geous personality of the "public enemy" has been shared to some degree by large numbers. This alone can explain the front pages of our newspapers. The sensational interest in crime is based not only on fear and disapproval but also on a profound unconscious admiration of achievement and courage, no matter how deplorable their outcome may be. These modern Robin Hoods and Rinaldo Rinaldinis appeal covertly to a people deeply imbued with an admiration for the adventurous spirit. The character of these "public enemies" is often romantically distorted by a tendency to exaggerate their courage and to ascribe to them a generosity they do not possess. I have been amazed at the extent to which young delinquents idealize their own criminality in the same way. One of them assured me that he would never hold up a poor man, and insisted vigorously on his own generosity. His greatest pleasure was to share the proceeds of his criminal exploits with others and by this magnanimity satisfied his longing for power and independence. Unconsciously he was a frightened boy crying for his mother's and older brother's help. His dreams gave disguised but unmistakable expression to his covert weakness and sense of dependence. The essential factor in his criminality represented his repudiation of incompetence and an attempt to prove what a "tough guy" he was.

The frequency of this type of conflict indicates that it must be based on a common factor in our civilization, namely the rapid transition from the expanding period of the Frontier to a standardized, industrialized, and mechanical life. The traditional admiration of adventure and personal achievement evokes individual initiative, but the conditions of contemporary existence do not reward it.

In such a situation the most vulnerable

group is obviously composed of those who are more dependent and passive than the average, for their attitude contradicts most flagrantly the group ideal of aggressive individualism. In their struggle against these objectionable weaknesses they become neurotics or criminals. They become criminals if other factors such as poor economic conditions, disrupted homes, and the bad example of other boys ... coöperate with these emotional factors. Contemporary life requires a readjustment of outlook, coöperation, and a certain amount of subordination inevitable in so complicated an economic system as our heterogeneous society. There is now a place and a need for more passive, contemplative, and artistic natures.

We conclude that an important factor in the spread of criminality in America is the discrepancy between traditional ideals and existing social conditions. An over-organized civilization requires, apart from individualistic virtues, a sense for coördination and order; and although the traditional ideals need not be abandoned, they must be modified and adjusted to new conditions if we wish them to help youth to accommodate themselves to the world as it is. Submission to order, a complicated system of laws, was unsuitable to the Frontier days when everything depended on courage and resourcefulness. Buffalo Bill and Jack London's heroes were not always defenders of law and order.

From this point of view modern crime appears as a new form of Quixotism. Just as Don Quixote exotically imitated the errant knight and became an insane criminal, our delinquent youth pursues the pioneer ideals of the Wild West and in the absence of Redskins attack their peaceful fellow citizens.

"The land of the free and the home of the brave" is in process of becoming a home of order. The development of this group ideal will contribute more to the solution of the problem of crime than the most refined methods of crime detection. Prevention is preferable to surgery and it is better to prevent criminal behavior by education than to rely alone upon public disposition of incurable criminals. As in medicine, prevention depends on a deeper and more thorough knowledge than therapy and therefore develops later. The prevention of crime by education will follow the social surgery of removing the criminal by imprisonment.

Another manifestation of the cultural lag is the wide spread of neurosis. There can be little doubt that this is caused by common factors and that its cause must be sought in general rather than in particular circumstances. No one with psychiatric experience can overlook the fact that a large portion of our urban population shows definite neurotic trends and the common features of their emotional disturbances must represent common cultural factors.

A specialist of emotional disturbances practicing at the present day in this country who attempts to help his patient by the method of psychoanalysis is inevitably impressed by the frequency of one kind of conflict. The patients are driven by a relentless competitiveness in any given field and are at the same time afraid and wearied by this strenuous life of race and struggle, are tortured by insecurity and secretly want in their hearts, more than anything else, rest and security. In the course of their analysis they disclose their strong desire for dependence, parental love and protection. This attitude is buried deeply in their unconscious, because their mature conscious self rejects it as a sign of softness. In defending themselves against this concealed passivity they rush more violently into the race of contemporary life and this competitiveness is by no means friendly and neighborly but hostile. It is not primarily a practical effort to eliminate a competitor but rather a desire to exhibit superiority and offset the shame felt for a deeply buried insecurity. It rests on a hate of others merely because they are or appear to be stronger, and is a competition for internal prestige which is injured by the unconscious wish for childish dependence. This conflict between aggressive ambition and longing for security we find as a central issue behind a great variety of neurotic symptoms, criminal behavior, and also emotionally caused organic disturbances. Particularly in certain gastro-intestinal disturbances this conflict situation is in the foreground. . . .

Those of us who have had the opportunity to study patients in other cultural environments are particularly impressed by the frequency and intensity of this conflict between ambition and dependence in present-day America. In most of our patients this conflict emerges as the core of their emotional life which outweighs all other problems of their human relationships. Not that in other cultures people do not suffer from the same conflict, for I have seen it often enough in patients of various races and countries. In America, however, it occurs more frequently as a central issue of the neurosis. A group of psychoanalysts recently distinguished themselves by emphasizing cultural factors in their patients' personalities and insisted that this conflict described above is peculiarly characteristic of western civilization, since personality was largely determined by its cultural environment. In contrast to this environmental view stands the more conservative conception that a universal human conflict is involved. As it is generally the case the truth is found between the two extremes. There is strong support for the view that the conflict between competitive self-assertion and dependence is universal and inherent in every form of social life, but its exceptional intensity and generality in America require special explanation.

The answer is to be found in the culturally determined internal inconsistency of our social standards; the traditional one-sided worship of individual success in a complex interdependent society and the exaggerated emphasis on independence in times of great insecurity. In the frank, intimate atmosphere of the analytic sessions, when pretensions fall and deceptive embellishments are discarded, the emotional structure of our society appears in its naked reality as it is reflected in a magnified fashion in the patient's strivings, hopes, disappointments, and anxieties. The prestige attached to independent achievement on the one hand and the longing for security, love, and belonging to somebody or some group on the other are the two poles between which patients are torn in a futile struggle.

After long hours of daily work, spent listening to the suffering victims of these unsettled times and trying to extract sense from the kaleidoscopic variety of sincere self-revelations, a hypnagogic vision appears before the eyes of the pondering psychoanalyst. The analyst sees his patients—physicians, lawyers, engineers, bankers, advertising men, teachers and laboratory research men of universities, students, and clerks—engaged in a Marathon race, their eager faces distorted by strain, their eyes focused not upon their goal, but upon each other with a mixture of hate, envy, and admiration. Panting and perspiring, they run and never arrive. They would all like to stop but dare not as long as the others are running. What makes them run so frantically, as though they were driven by the threatening swish of an invisible whip wielded by an invisible slave driver? The driver and the whip they carry in their own minds. If one of them finally stops and begins leisurely to whistle a tune or watch a passing cloud or picks up a stone and with childish curiosity turns it around in his hand, they all look upon him at first with astonishment and then with contempt and disgust. They call him names, a dreamer or a parasite, a theoretician or a schizophrenic, and above all, an effeminate. They not only do not understand him—they not only despise him but "they hate him as their own sin." All of them would like to stop—ask each other questions, sit down to a chat about futilities—they all would like to belong to each other because they all feel desperately alone—chasing on in a never-ending chase. They do not dare to stop until the rest stop lest they lose all their self-respect, because they know only one value—that of running—running for its own sake.

The vision of the Marathon runners without an Athens to reach vanishes and a group of western amazons appears on the scene. They are healthier-looking than the men in the exhausted running crowd, self-possessed and cool—they do not wear armor and carry a spear, but wear a sweater and carry a tennis racket. They watch the running and perspiring crowd of men with a mixture of amusement and contempt—shrug their shoulders and sigh with resignation. Then they bathe and sit for hours before the mirror, dress, read, listen to or play music and card games, exercise, drink tea or whiskey, and make desperate attempts not to be reminded of their physiology or anatomy as women. This is the way they can protect themselves from inescapable frustration. They are living in a civilization that has not only no time for creativeness, but considers the biological creativeness of women as a nuisance and impediment in the racing, and in which there is nothing more contemptuous than being a "sissy".

Can a civilization survive where discontent and frustration are so oppressive and extensive and in which men are driven toward the goal of an extinct period, engaged in futile and exhausting efforts to live up to unattainable standards of individualism? A civilization in which women become frigid and masculine in order to protect themselves from inevitable frustration and are attached to exhausted, blindly competing mates whose sole concern is to hide from themselves and others their desperate sense of insecurity and their dread that they will not make the grade in the race of life? A solution can be found only in redirecting energy to creative goals vital to contemporary society and attainable within it. The economic conquest of America is nearly accomplished and the practical exploitation of the basic inventions on a large scale well-nigh exhausted. And even though some technical innovations are still to be expected, the economic field is near to its saturation point and will no longer provide sufficient outlet for creative ambition and so becomes the arena of destructive competition. Are there new frontiers—open territories worthy of the individualistic and productive forces of a great nation?

NEIL LEONARD (b. 1927) received his Ph.D. from Harvard University in American Civilization. He teaches at the University of Pennsylvania and specializes in the literature, art, and music of the United States since 1885. *Jazz and the White Americans* (1962) is a study of the 1920s conflict between jazz and the guardians of traditional morals and the supporters of classical and romantic music. How did an essentially esthetic question become linked to social and moral issues? How did the fear of jazz heighten racial tensions?*

Neil Leonard

Traditionalist Opposition to Jazz

In 1922, when the jazz controversy was coming to a head, J. Hartley Manners' play *The National Anthem* opened on Broadway. The plot depicted naive young people ignoring the counsel of a wise traditionalist parent and debauching themselves into decadence. Manners dramatized the way jazz stimulated the youth's downfall, and in his Foreword argued that the new music was "modern man's saturnalia." Throughout the play jazz not only undermined the morality of susceptible young people, but also threatened all civilization, which, if the jazz age continued unchecked, seemed doomed to barbarism. Many people who saw *The National Anthem* shared Manners' fears about jazz. Journalist Bruce

Bliven described the audience at one performance as resembling a group of indignantly wide-eyed members of "the Ladies' Auxiliary of Flushing, L.I. assembled to hear a lecture on the white slave traffic." He further reported that jazz had become a burning issue among many middle-class people in New York and its suburbs.

The National Anthem and the fears it helped to provoke indicate the nature and the amount of agitation aroused by the jazz dispute. Such excitement over music on the part of so many Americans was extraordinary. Previously music had caused relatively little excitement because it seemed largely irrelevant to practical matters. Most Americans thought

*From Neil Leonard, *Jazz and the White Americans* (Chicago: The University of Chicago Press, 1962), pp. 29–46. © 1962 by The University of Chicago. Reprinted without footnotes by permission.

of it in terms of entertainment, often pleasant but of minor importance. Even traditional academic music, which the arbiters of musical taste urged upon the public as a strong social and moral force, seemed to have little to do with the pressing concerns of most people. But after World War I many Americans began to take music more seriously, when they found that jazz was strongly connected with social and moral problems which could not be ignored. These social and moral implications made the jazz controversy part of the bitter conflict between the relative norms which were gaining currency and traditional, absolute values.

Upheld chiefly by Protestant, middle-class Americans of Anglo-Saxon ancestry, traditional values demanded among other things belief in moral and metaphysical idealism, confidence in the individual's capacity for self-directed growth toward intelligence and high purpose, and faith in the progress of civilization. For some time, traditionalists were becoming increasingly alarmed at the threats to their values posed by relative norms that were fast making inroads into American society. After the Armistice traditionalists were fully aroused for a militant counterattack on what they saw as a rising tide of degeneration. Many of them regarded jazz, along with intemperance and unconventional sexual behavior, as a sign or a cause of the advancing degeneration and assailed the new music as a major vice.

To understand these assaults, it is important first to know what traditionalists meant by the word jazz. After the Armistice few of them differentiated between real and commercial jazz. Anything that sounded even faintly like jazz (in other words, that had one or more of a variety of recognizable jazz characteristics) they called "jazz." Therefore it seems best to refer to this jazzlike music as "jazz"—

surrounding the word with quotation marks, as traditionalists often did.

The statuses of the opponents of "jazz" depended, in varying degrees, on traditional values. There were two groups of opponents. The first included guardians of traditional morals and manners: clergymen, educators, and other community leaders, certain business and professional men, and politicians. The second group embraced people economically dependent upon, or esthetically committed to, traditional music: musicians, music critics, music teachers, dancing teachers, patrons, and lovers of traditional music. These and others influenced by them disliked "jazz" for several reasons.

To begin with, it seemed grossly to violate traditional musical values, particularly those of academic music, which defined for many of the cultivated and their emulators what music should be. D. G. Mason summed up the musical criteria of such traditionalists: "The truth is, our whole view of music was based on the style of classic and romantic symphonists beginning with Haydn and Mozart and ending with Mendelssohn and Schumann." The traditionalists' esthetic principles grew out of the romantic philosophy of art. . . . Howard Mumford Jones has conveniently summarized them: Art was the expression of the highest idealism, which might be interpreted as purposefulness in the life of the cosmos, soul, or state. Art of both the classic and romantic schools was acceptable in so far as it expressed the highest morality, which was nobility. However, the danger of the romantic school was that it could lead to excess or formlessness. The notion of art as a discipline demanding restraint and craftsmanship was central.

Upholders of these values found "jazz" so strange that it could scarcely be called music. Dr. Henry Van Dyke, a prominent Presbyterian clergyman and a professor at Princeton, declared "As I understand ["jazz"], it is not music at all." For many it seemed full of wild excesses and formlessness, totally lacking in restraint and discipline. Music critic Sigmund Spaeth called it "merely a raucous and inarticulate shouting of hoarse-throated instruments, with each player trying to outdo his fellows, in fantastic cacophony." In an article entitled "Back to Pre-War Morals," in the *Ladies' Home Journal,* journalist John R. McMahon wrote, "If Beethoven should return to earth and witness the doings of [a "jazz"] orchestra, he would thank heaven for his deafness. . . . All this music had a droning, jerky incoherence interrupted with a spasmodic 'blah!! blah!!' that reminded me of the way that live sheep are turned into mutton." Thomas A. Edison was quoted as saying he preferred to play "jazz" records backward because they sounded better that way.

Most traditionalists seem to have agreed with concert pianist Ashley Pettis that "jazz is nothing more or less than the distortion of every esthetic principle." Walter R. Spaulding, a professor of music at Harvard, observed that "jazz" was "exciting" but good music "must surely have many other qualities such as . . . sublimity and ideality." Frequently traditionalists complained that "jazz" lacked soul or purposefulness in the life of the soul. Walter Damrosch charged, "Jazz . . . is rhythm without . . . soul." A *New York Times* writer was more explicit about the traditionalist spiritual feelings which jazz failed to evoke.

With music of the old style, even the most moving, the listener was seldom upset from his dignified posture. When listening to Tchaikovsky's "March Slav," perhaps he might feel a tingling starting at his heels and lifting the roof of his head clear up to the ceiling, as though his ectoplasm—as the spiritualists call the spirit substance—had suddenly broken free from its mortal container and was up in the open spaces of the auditorium looping the loop and nose-diving. Yet the bodily anchor remained intact. The listener behaved as impassively as the radio's microphone. Nothing in his manner indicated either a struggle for self-control or an absence of decorum. The perturbation spent itself internally.

Far from spending itself in the life of the soul or the spirit, jazz seemed to provoke man's "lower nature," the carnal. John Philip Sousa objected that "jazz" "employs primitive rhythms which excite the basic human instincts." Others complained that the new music had the same effect on the brain as alcohol: A New York physician, Dr. E. Elliot Rawlings, explained, "Jazz music causes drunkenness . . . [by sending] a continuous whirl of impressionable stimulations to the brain, producing thoughts and imaginations which overpower the will. Reason and reflection are lost and the actions of the persons are directed by the stronger animal passions."

The bodily movements which "jazz" elicited seemed to be further evidence of the way the intoxicating sounds of the new music brought out man's lower nature—in ways that reminded traditionalists of the behavior of "inferior" races. H. O. Osgood, an editor of *The Musical Courier,* described the movements of the Ted Lewis Band as a kind of savage rite with "all the players jolting up and down and writhing about in simulated ecstasy, in the manner of Negroes at a Southern camp-meeting afflicted with religious frenzy." A New Jersey Supreme Court Justice J. F. Minturn charged that, "In response to ["jazz's"] call there ensues a series of snake-like gyrations and weird contortions of seemingly agonized bodies and limbs, resembling an Asiatic *pot pourri* which . . . is called a dance."

The sensual appeal of "jazz" collided with traditionalist ideas of sex. In *Race and Nationality in American Life* Oscar Handlin summarized these ideas: The spiritual union of married adults for purposes of procreation was the only acceptable occasion for sexual intercourse. Frequent indulgence or masturbation, the results of animal passion, were said to bring on illness, shorten life, and breed degenerate progeny. Furthermore, most people in the government, the medical profession, and the clergy viewed birth control and abortion as crimes against the state, nature, and God. The law in sexual matters was self-restraint.

Jazz seemed to fly in the face of this repression. Fenton T. Bott, head of the traditionalist National Association of Masters of Dancing, charged in 1921, "those moaning saxophones and the rest of the instruments with their broken, jerky rhythm make a purely sensual appeal. They call out the low and rowdy instincts. All of us dancing teachers know this to be a fact. . . . Jazz is the very foundation and essence of salacious dancing." *The Catholic Telegraph* of Cincinnati complained, "the music is sensuous, the embracing of partners . . . is absolutely indecent; and the motions—they are such that as may not be described with any respect for propriety in a family newspaper. Suffice it to say that there are certain houses appropriate for such dances but those houses have been closed by law." Other religious periodicals denounced "jazz" dances as "impure," "polluting," and "debasing."

Moreover, traditionalists often believed that the feelings "jazz" evoked were not confined to the dance hall. Miss Alice Barrow, who had worked for a number of educational and welfare institutions as a teacher and investigator, made a study of the evil results of "jazz" in mid-Western towns and she warned parents that:

The nature of the music and the crowd psychology working together bring to many individuals an unwholesome excitement. Boy-and-girl couples leave the hall in a state of dangerous disturbance. Any worker who has gone into the night to gather the facts of activities outside the dance hall is appalled, first of all perhaps, by the blatant disregard of even the elementary rules of civilization. . . . We must expect a few casualties in social intercourse, but the modern dance is producing little short of holocaust. The statistics of illegitimacy in this country show a great increase in recent years.

Other traditionalists delivered still darker warnings. A New York Episcopal rector, Percy Grant, cautioned his congregation about the evils of "jazz" by reading from a leaflet which said that 65,000 girls had disappeared from the United States in 1921 "without leaving a trace." The rector told his parishioners to remember this if they forgot everything else he had said. A report of the Illinois Vigilance Association, led by the Reverend Phillip Yarrow, was equally disturbing. Its agents found that in 1921–22 jazz had caused the downfall of 1,000 girls in Chicago alone.

Objections raised against words of "jazz" songs supported complaints that the music was vulgar and sensual. Fenton T. Bott, the dancing teacher, who charged that "jazz" music had a sensual appeal said, "The words also are very suggestive, thinly veiling immoral ideas." Other people went further, avowing that the words were downright vulgar. In 1920 Mrs. Marx Obendorfer, national music chairman of the General Federation of Women's Clubs, told members of the federation that "jazz" lyrics were "unspeakable" and that "ninety per cent of [them] would not be allowed to go through the mails if [they] were literature." The following year in an article entitled, "Does Jazz Put the Sin in Syncopation?" Mrs. Obendorfer reported that the music supervisor of a large urban high school had examined the lyrics of over 2,000 "best selling" songs and had deemed only forty "fit for boys and girls to sing together."

Traditionalists found that the circumstances surrounding "jazz" and the people who played it offered evidence of the evil nature of the music. Insisting that "everything must be judged by the company it keeps and attracts," Will Earhart, music director of the School of Education at the University of Pittsburgh, observed that the works of traditional composers "are heard in certain places and received by a certain clientele gathered there. They seem to be appropriate to the places in which they are heard, and to the people who gather to hear them. So does 'Jazz.'" An editorial in *Etude* declared, "Jazz, at its worst, is often associated with vile surroundings, filthy words, unmentionable dances and obscene plays with which respectable Americans are so disgusted that they turn with dismay at the mere mention of 'Jazz,' which they naturally blame for the whole fearful caravan of vice and near-vice."

Probably the most damaging association of "jazz" was its identification with the brothel, usually the Negro brothel. The music critic of the *New York Herald Tribune*, H. E. Krehbiel, who had been interested in other types of music connected with the Negro, was disgusted by such a lewd association, and he feared that more "jazz" and foul dances were "soon to emanate from the Negro brothels of the South." Jazz clarinetist Milton Mezzrow wrote that in the twenties, "Our music was

called 'nigger music' and 'whorehouse music' and 'nice' people turned up their noses at it."

The most disturbing thing about the new music was that it seemed to infect almost every part of American life. A. W. Beaven, a minister in Rochester, New York, explained, "It has gotten beyond the dance and the music and is now an attitude toward life in general. We are afflicted with a moral and spiritual anemia." Bringing out man's lower nature in a number of ways ranging from crime and suicide to the break-up of the home, jazz seemed to strike at the very heart of the traditional way of life. Dr. John R. Straton, a Baptist clergyman in New York and the chief spokesman for Fundamentalism after the death of William Jennings Bryan, argued, "I have no patience with this modern jazz tendency, whether it be in music, science, social life or religion. It is part of the lawless spirit which is being manifested in many departments of life, endangering our civilization in its general revolt against authority and established order." Dr. Francis E. Clark, president of the Christian Endeavor Society, called jazz dancing "an offence against womanly purity, the very fountainhead of our family and civil life."

Traditionalists were particularly disturbed at the way "jazz" was infecting the minds of children. Sherwood Boblitz in *The Musician* warned of "one fact, which is too vile and too glaring to longer go unnoticed and uncommented upon: the only music that many children and adults are ever able to hear . . . [is] generally ragtime and tawdry at that." And Mrs. Elise F. White, a musician, writer, and active New England clubwoman, observed that generally children had little interest in academic music. They preferred "ragtime" and demanded, "What good is all this high-class music, anyhow, except just to harrow up your feelings? Let's play something lively."

It was difficult to arrest this tendency, for young people appeared particularly susceptible to "jazz." In 1925 the author of the *Etude* editorial, "Is Jazz the Pilot of Disaster?" cautioned, "Jazz is doing a vast amount of harm to young minds and bodies not yet developed to resist evil temptation." The orchestra leader of the state hospital at Napa, California, declared, "I can say from my own knowledge that about fifty percent of our young boys and girls from the age 16 to 25 that land in the insane asylum these days are jazz-crazy dope fiends and public dance hall patrons. Jazz combinations—dope fiends and public dance halls—are all the same, 'one.' Where you find one you will find the other." The extent to which some people feared the corruption of untrained minds by "jazz" is illustrated in the brief of the Salvation Army of Cincinnati, which in 1926 obtained a temporary court injunction, preventing construction of a movie theater next to one of its homes for expectant mothers. The plaintiff argued, "We are loathe to believe that babies born in the maternity hospital are to be legally subjected to the implanting of jazz emotions by such enforced proximity to a theater and jazz palace."

Traditionalist concepts of race bore strongly upon the opposition to jazz. Many traditionalists seem to have agreed with well-known actress Laurette Taylor (who played a lead in her husband's play, *The National Anthem)* when she said, "Jazz, the impulse for wildness that has undoubtedly come over many things besides the music of this country, is traceable to the Negro influence." . . .

Traditionalist notions about the origins of jazz provided fuel for these racial fears. Whereas some traditionalists believed that jazz was born in the Negro brothel, others traced the origins of the music to the jungle and believed that the African roots of "jazz" explained its association with violence. Mrs. Marx Obendorfer argued that, "Jazz originally was the accompaniment of the voodoo dancer, stimulating the half-crazed barbarian to the vilest deeds. . . . [It] has also been employed by other barbaric people to stimulate brutality and sensuality." Such notions helped spread fears that Negroes under the influence of "jazz" would become violent. Negro jazz clarinetist Buster Bailey pointed out that during the years when he first played professionally, whites were afraid "we'd go after their women."

Many traditionalists found that the African origins of "jazz" held even more frightening implications. "The consensus of opinion of leading medical and other scientific authorities," wrote Dr. Florence Richards, medical director of a Philadelphia high school for girls, "is that its influence is as harmful and degrading to civilized races as it always has been among savages from whom we borrowed it." She warned that continued exposure to this evil influence "may tear to pieces our whole social fabric." Others believed that "jazz," the music of the jungle, was a form of retrogression that was returning American society to an age of barbarism. Not only science but history as well lent credence to such fears. Appalled at the prospect of Americans "reduced to the low state of inferior races now on this planet," a biologist exhorted, "better extinction than a decline to the savage past. Jazz is a signboard on the road that was travelled by Greece and Rome. Orgies of lewd dancing preceded the downfall of those nations." Either as a cause or as a symbol, Negro jazz threatened to turn back the clock of civilized progress.

Just as "jazz" was objectionable because

it conflicted with the standards of traditional music, the jazz man was disturbing because he did not conform to the pattern followed by the traditional musician.

The traditionalist concept of idealism, interpreted to mean purposefulness in the life of the cosmos, implied God's guidance in the esthetic expression of universal truths. Part of the artist's proper inspiration was a kind of emotion, which traditionalists called "passion," the longing for the ideal world of perfection. In the attainment of this ideal the discipline of restraint and craftsmanship was basic. A music teacher's monthly magazine like *The Musician* printed numerous articles which reiterated the "success" pattern and held up for emulation by the young student the early strivings of famous musicians. Such examples showed that to become an artist required pluck, diligence, and persistence during years of patient training in the established tradition of the concert stage.

Traditionalists worried because jazz men ignored or flouted these ideas. Walter Damrosch felt that jazz men lacked proper inspiration, "real emotion which . . . might give life to their music." Far too many young musicians seemed little concerned with the discipline that accompanied "real emotion," or "passion." Mrs. Elise F. White argued that the coming generation, preoccupied as it was, with such baubles as "rag-time," failed to concern itself with "real" music, "which demands much time and thought; the music of artistic cultivation, of humble ambitions, prayerfully and earnestly followed; of obedience to teachers; of self-denial, renunciation and sacrifice; of the worship of beauty, and the passionate desire to express it."

Because jazz men had not been trained in traditional discipline, traditionalists called them incompetent. The "Topics of the [New York] *Times*" column compared "jazz" with the "new poetry," and concluded "both are the products, not of innovators, but of incompetents. The maker of jazz would compose music if he could . . . and had something to say." And what could be more indicative of the jazz musician's incompetence than the fact that he frequently turned to academic music for his material. Walter Damrosch's brother, Frank, an influential musician in his own right, charged that jazzing the classics was "not only an outrage on beautiful music, but also a confession of poverty, of inability to compose music of any value."

Moreover, "jazz" threatened the growth of traditional music by spoiling the musician's desire for "proper" training and performance. Walter Damrosch argued, "Undoubtedly it stifles the true musical instinct, turning away many of our talented young people from the persistent, continued study and execution of good music." In addition, "jazz" spoiled the prospective musician's technique. "To become an artist on any wind instrument is work of a lifetime," explained bandmaster Edwin Franko Goldman. He warned that the "grotesque effects" of the new music ruined the player's intonation. H. E. Krehbiel complained that "the principal characteristic of jazz is a vulgar sliding from tone to tone [which caused an] . . . unnatural contortion of the lips and forcing of the breath," thus unfitting the performer for playing academic music.

Although traditionalists took great pain to point to the evil "jazz" was working in American moral and musical development, few of them specified precisely what characteristics of the music were causing the trouble. It seems safe to say, however that some traditionalists found virtually any non-traditional jazz element or practice to be offensive.

Twentieth-century academic musicians seldom, if ever, improvised, and many of them condemned improvisation, which flourished in jazz. Frank Patterson, an editor of *The Musical Courier,* polled a number of academic musicians and reported that "They all agreed that the 'ad libbing' or 'jazzing' of a piece is thoroughly objectionable, and several of them advanced the opinion that this Bolshevistic smashing of the rules and tenets of decorous music, this excessive freedom of interpretation, tended to a similar letting down on the part of the dancers, a similar disregard for the self-contained and self-restrained attitude that has been prescribed by the makers of the rules of dignified social intercourse."

The rhythm of jazz was disturbing also. Daniel Gregory Mason called it "formally inane" and "mechanically repeated." Will Earhart charged that jazz "represents, in its convulsive, twitching, hiccoughing rhythms, the abdication of control by the central nervous system—the brain."

Equally objectionable were the strange "staccato tempi," "curlicues," "rasps," "cries," and "laughs" and the sounds of such "nerve-wracking devices" as "cow bells, rattles, and fog horns" which seemed conducive to immorality. The "plaintive and pleading notes of the violin and clarinet, the imploring tones of the saxophone" seemed to lead to drunkenness and the overpowering of the will. The "moaning" saxophones were said to increase the "sensual appeal" of jazz and to bring out "low and rowdy instincts." Some elements of "jazz" were even said to impair health. The Health Commissioner of Milwaukee, Dr. George C. Ruhland, maintained that they excited "the nervous system until a veritable

hysterical frenzy is reached. It is easy to see that such a frenzy is damaging to the nervous system and will undermine the health in no time."

Traditionalists combatted the evils of "jazz" in several ways. First, a number of persons associated with traditional music and dance joined what a *New York Times* article called "The Conspiracy of Silence against Jazz." The conspirators worked on the theory that the "least said soonest mended." Their policy was to fight evil with good. For example, the superintendent of the Des Moines, Iowa, schools noted that his music department said "practically nothing about jazz. Instead there is a carefully planned program . . . and definite music appreciation instruction which seems to offset the crudities of the jazz madness."

Another tactic was to describe "jazz" as a dying fad. The author of *In His Steps,* Charles M. Sheldon, was one of those who assured lovers of "good" music that "jazz" had lost its appeal. Still others dismissed "jazz" as a burlesque of "real" music. Violinist Fritz Kreisler, then living in New York, explained, "We do not think of pen and ink caricatures as art. Jazz has the same relationship to music." Traditionalists also tried to tarnish the popularity of the new music by ridicule. For instance, the *New York Times* printed articles headed "Jazz Frightens Bears" and "Cornetist to Queen Victoria Falls Dead on Hearing Coney Island Jazz Band."

Still other traditionalists took organized action. In 1919 the National Association of Dancing Masters opened a campaign to reform dancing in America. At its convention in New York the association passed a resolution urging members not to "permit vulgar dancing and cheap jazz music to be played. . . . After all what is dancing but an interpretation of the music." The association sought the co-operation of churches and it printed booklets condemning "jazz," as well as a chart illustrating the approved dance steps. This material went to schools, dancing teachers, and dance halls with the commendation of the United States Public Health Service, which distributed it to thousands of welfare agencies.

In 1921 the music section of the General Federation of Women's Clubs launched a crusade against "jazz." The president of the musical section of the General Federation urged that never before had America so needed the help and inspiration of "good" music and concluded, "Let us carry out this motto in every home in America firmly, steadfastly, until all the music in our land becomes an influence for the good." Two years later at its national convention delegates of the 2,000,000-member federation voted to "annihilate" the new music.

The Federal Interdepartmental Social Hygiene Board issued reports on the evils "jazz" was working in small towns. The board co-operated with the dancing masters and women's clubs and planned to enlarge the Public Welfare Department of Illinois in order to check the "jazz" cancer where it was spreading most rapidly.

In 1922 the Ninth Recreational Congress convened at Atlantic City and resolved to war on "jazz" with better songs which would embody "the finer ideals of American life." Professor Peter Dykeman, of the University of Wisconsin, a well-known authority on music, led the reform committee, which included music critic Sigmund Spaeth as well as the director of the Philadelphia Music League, and an official of the Bureau of Community Music of the Community Services. Three years later Henry Ford opened a drive

against the new music by sponsoring a series of traditional folk dances which he hoped would counteract the evils of "jazz" dancing. A group of influential Episcopal churchwomen in New York, including Mrs. J. P. Morgan, Mrs. Borden Harriman, Mrs. Henry Phipps, Mrs. James Roosevelt, and Mrs. E. H. Harriman, proposed an organization to discourage "excess of nudity" and "improper ways of dancing."

Some traditionalists suggested government prohibition. In a speech before 1,000 teachers, the superintendent of schools in Kansas City, Missouri, warned "This nation has been fighting booze for for a long time. I am just wondering whether jazz isn't going to have to be legislated against as well." In 1922 the New York State Legislature passed the Cotillo Bill, which empowered the Commissioner of Licenses of New York City to regulate "jazz" and dancing. He promptly banned both on Broadway after midnight. By 1929, at least sixty communities, including Cleveland, Detroit, Kansas City, Omaha, and Philadelphia, had regulations prohibiting "jazz" in public dance halls. . . .

By the mid-twenties it was becoming increasingly clear that the appeal of "jazz" was growing in spite of traditionalist opposition. In the face of this realization, and in view of growing evidence that the evil elements of the music were being refined or filtered out, the frontal attack which sought to banish "jazz" lost strength. At the same time there emerged an effort to restrict the development and popularity of the new music. Morroe Berger points out that opponents of "jazz" attempted to fix its esthetic value and social prestige below the worth and position of academic music. This policy resulted in tolerance of the new music as long as it remained in its "proper place." Dean Smith of the Yale Music School spoke for those traditionalists who sought not to kill "jazz" but to confine it to its "proper" sphere. In an article, "Putting Jazz in Its Place," he argued that "Any criticism of its music or of its composers is academic and uncalled for—provided jazz holds to its original purpose of entertaining people in their times of recreation." This meant that "jazz" in any form was to stay out of the concert hall. "The development of art music," explained Ashley Pettis, "is separate and distinct from the work of so-called jazz exponents. . . . It is all right in its place—the cabaret and the dance hall—but it should not be allowed to invade the sacred precinct of our concert halls."

Furthermore, jazz men were to leave "classical" music alone. In 1927 the 400,000 women organized in the National Federation of Music Clubs launched an effort to fight "jazzing of the noble compositions of the great composers." Commenting on this move, an editorial in the *New York Times* pointed out that one purpose of the clubs was "to keep modern music in its place." It was permissible, the editorial continued, for "jazz" "to snort and jangle in night clubs, dance halls and on the musical comedy stage. But it must keep its brassy hands off the classics, or walking delegates from the music clubs will do something official."

An examination of the traditionalists' response to jazz suggests that values primarily esthetic are interrelated with those chiefly social or moral, that groups of people with different manners and morals tend to associate themselves with different styles or forms of art, and that any attempt to introduce the musical values of one group into the musical life of a different group is a difficult or impossible operation. Since the musical and non-musical values of supporters of jazz differed from those of traditionalists, it is not surprising that traditionalists rejected jazz. The strongest opposition came from those whose status depended most heavily on conventional values, people like the Reverend Mr. Straton, Mr. Bott, and Mrs. Obendorfer. Their values were so deeply rooted and so inflexible that an esthetic novelty like jazz aroused distaste and fear that forced strong opposition. Ironically the intense opposition to jazz unified its supporters and ultimately helped it gain a firm place in the sensibilities of many Americans.

A native of Terre Haute, Indiana, DAVID A.
SHANNON (b. 1920) was granted a doctorate from
the University of Wisconsin. He has taught at Columbia
Teachers College, the University of Wisconsin, the
University of Maryland, Rutgers University, and
presently is Professor of History and Dean of the
Faculty of Arts and Sciences at the University of
Virginia. Although his specialty is recent American
political history, in his *Between the Wars: America,
1919–1941* Shannon includes a judicious sketch of
developments in art during the 1920s. How did the
prosperity of the decade benefit the arts? To what
extent did this prosperity free the artist to explore
new avenues of creativity?*

David A. Shannon

The Progress of Modern Painting

Prosperity was a basic fact of the 1920's, one that shaped and conditioned many aspects of life outside the economic realm. A generally expanding economy underlay a generally expansive view about life, as happened again in the generation after World War II. To say that the economy was healthy would be to ignore the almost fatal illness that struck it low in 1929, but it was clearly prosperous. . . .

America's affluence during the 1920's underlay the more widespread interest in art. Original paintings of merit, with relatively few exceptions, hung only on the walls of the homes of the very rich before World War I. Some of the millionaires bought widely, it is true, and they caused some consternation in Europe lest they deplete the continent of its art masterpieces. But not until the 1920's did any significant number of people of only moderate wealth purchase art for their homes beyond perhaps a portrait of a family member or prints of sentimental subjects. Affluence also made possible the establishment of more art museums. Sixty new museums opened in American cities during the 1920's.

Interest in American art, and even contemporary painting, however, was still relatively slight. In 1927 the Irish-American collector John Quinn sold his magnificent collection of recent French and American painting for $700,000. By midcentury, the Quinn collection would have brought millions. But there was

*From David A. Shannon, *Between the Wars: America, 1919–1941* (Boston: Houghton Mifflin Company, 1965), pp. 85–101. Reprinted by permission.

some market for the products of contemporary painters. At least several serious painters managed to make a living throughout the decade. Not all Americans were as ignorant of American art as President Coolidge who, when asked by the French government in 1925 to send an exhibit of contemporary American painting to an international show in Paris, replied that the United States would have to pass up the affair because it did not have any painters.

Actually, American painting was in something of a ferment and had been for almost a decade before the United States entered the war. The United States, of course, like any society, had always had a certain number of professional painters, and some of them were artists of distinction. By the early twentieth century, however, a group of painters in New York known collectively as the Academy had managed to get almost a monopoly on exhibitions of American painting. Some members of the Academy were able technicians, but their work was seldom exciting and was thoroughly conventional. Two groups, one a small set of realists led by Robert Henri and another of modernists who might be said to have been led by the photographer Alfred Stieglitz, broke the grip that the Academy had on art and set the art world aflame.

In 1908 Henri and seven of his friends and students, who came to be known as The Eight or the Ash Can School, managed to present an exhibition in New York at a private gallery. Not strikingly different from Academy painters in technique, The Eight departed from convention primarily in their subject matter, which usually was ordinary people and ordinary sights of city life. They did not often actually paint ash cans, but the term did suggest their emphasis. Of The Eight, John Sloan became the best known,

although George Bellows, who was in the same tradition but not of the original group, became even more widely known and respected.

The Armory Art Show of 1913, which appeared in New York, Chicago, and Boston and which had been organized by the group of painters who made Stieglitz's studio on Fifth Avenue their headquarters, had an impact greater than The Eight. A huge exhibition, the Armory Show included works by French modernists of various kinds, all of whom took considerable liberties with surface reality or appearances in their painting and some of whom, the cubists for example, came close to abstraction. The Armory Show caused a tremendous furor. Conventional art critics even asserted that the artists' purpose was to overturn morality and Christianity. Former President Theodore Roosevelt denounced the exhibition. But to artists, especially young ones, the show had an enormously stimulating effect. Many young painters adopted the techniques and styles of the French *avant-garde,* a few art patrons became interested, and American art was never again the same.

During the dollar decade the American modernists were more in the limelight than the realists, just as in literary circles Proust and Joyce enjoyed a greater vogue than the "slice of life" school that derived from Zola. It would be difficult to get unanimity about a list of the outstanding modernist American painters of the 1920's, but John Marin, Georgia O'Keeffe, Max Weber, and the "cubist-realist" group, Charles Demuth, Charles Sheeler, and Joseph Stella, were certainly painters of top quality and representative of modernist painting of the decade. Marin, who became very well known before his death in 1953, was in his most abstract stage of development in the 1920's. Best known for his water colors, Marin painted New York City and Maine coastal scenes that were recognizable but distorted. Weber, who likewise had his greatest following after World War II, painted in a variety of styles, usually drawing strongly upon contemporary trends in Paris. Miss O'Keeffe, who married Stieglitz, employed a hard, clean line that was almost photographic, even when she was at her most abstract. Demuth, Sheeler, and Stella were midway between the kind of cubism that was popular in Paris before the war and realism. Their paintings were representational, but they emphasized the geometric forms of their subject matter, which often was a building or a machine or a bridge, distorting appearances to give their work a greater impression of reality. Some of their work, in fact, resembled the "art photography" of those who sought out intricate and geometric interplays of light and shadow.

Although the modernists attracted more attention, the realists continued to work in their tradition throughout the decade. Bellows became quite well known before his death in 1925, when he was still in his early forties, because of the subjects of his canvases and his own background. He had been an athlete, one of the star infielders of the Ohio State baseball team, before he began to study with Henri, and he frequently painted athletes. His boxing pictures especially were popular.

When one says that Bellows was popular it must be remembered that the term is relative. He was more popular than most serious painters, but to the great majority of Americans he was entirely unknown. Art in the formal sense was unimportant to most people. Most people lived out their days without ever seeing a great picture, little knowing or caring about the gap in their lives. To most people art was something you bought at a furniture store when you refurnished a room or the covers of *The Saturday Evening Post,* homey, sentimental things designed to evoke a chuckle or a sigh.

One of the most distinguished writers and editors of recent time, BERNARD A. DEVOTO (1897–1955) was a Harvard graduate, a teacher and lecturer, and winner of both the Pulitzer Prize for history and the Bancroft Prize. His list of books on American history and literature includes *Mark Twain's America* (1932) and *Across the Wide Missouri* (1947). In *The Literary Fallacy* (1944) DeVoto sharply criticized the writers of the Twenties for failing to recognize the dignity of man and for voicing a negativism that DeVoto felt would eventually lead to cynicism, heartbreak, and neurotic collapse. In light of the literary viewpoint expressed in this lecture, why does DeVoto suggest Sinclair Lewis as possibly the best novelist of the decade? Why does the critic argue that Hemingway's fiction has little to do with the real world? Why does he not find the characters of Hemingway or Dos Passos tragic?*

Bernard A. DeVoto

A Literary Waste Land

. . . I cannot take you through the literature of a decade in one lecture. I propose merely to examine the evidence of certain illustrations which seem to me to exhibit a relationship and a rough kind of harmony. They are all from the main current of the decade's literature, the official literature, the literature praised by writers themselves. They are also, whether consciously or unconsciously, within the final limitations imposed by the literary fallacy.

Sinclair Lewis will be remembered as the author of four novels, *Main Street,* *Babbitt, Arrowsmith,* and *Elmer Gantry.* Our purpose would permit us to approach them in a number of ways. We might say that their rationale shows a progressive shift from the ideas of Mr. Van Wyck Brooks to those of Mr. H. L. Mencken. We might say that their description of America is considerably more sociological than anything we have previously considered. We might say that although they show an energetic repudiation of American experience it is not an irreconcilable repudiation or even a fundamental one. We certainly ought to say that they have a greater gusto than any other fiction of the period. They are first-rate novels, and Mr. Lewis may well be the best novelist of the decade. But I have time only to inquire whether something which they lack may not be a common, and significant, lack in the literature of the period as a whole. I propose merely to inquire what Mr. Lewis's novels praise.

The critics have never been sure whether Mr. Lewis was trying to truly represent the life of his time or to caricature it, and it seems likely that Mr. Lewis has shared their uncertainty. Satire, however, has as important prerogative. So long as we understand what a satirist is driving at, we cannot ask him to tell the whole truth about it. The faithful representation of reality which other kinds of novelists hold to be their highest duty lays no obligation on him. But also there is a touchstone to satire: it has points of reference which make its values clear. Thus the spirited portraiture in *Main Street* withholds you from asking whether some aspects of life in Gopher Prairie may not have been distorted or ignored until you wonder what the town is being held against for reference. You discover that the reference is to certain adolescent ideas of Carol Kennicott. And suddenly it appears that the Village Virus which has poisoned America consists of the failure of small towns to support productions of the one-act plays of Eugene O'Neill, to provide candlelight at dinner, and to sanction lounging pajamas as evening wear for housewives. The superb evocation of the city of Zenith in *Babbitt* distracts one from values until one comes to consider the side of George F. Babbitt with whom Mr. Lewis finally developed a warm friendship and to consider the few inhabitants of the city who are held to be living the good life. Whereupon there appears so trivial an imagination

of deep experience, so shallow and unsophisticated a conception of emotional relationships and intellectual activity, that one sees at once what has been left out of Zenith. What has been left out is human profundity, whether admirable or base.

Finally, when a novelist creates heroes he comes out into the open. Mr. Lewis's understanding is illuminated for us by *Arrowsmith*. Here he not only undertakes to make a sociologist's survey of the entire field of medicine in America; he also undertakes to exalt the scientific ideal and to priase a way of life which he thinks of as heroic. We may dismiss the survey as within the prerogatives of satire, though Mr. Lewis's virtuosity blinds one to the ferocious injustice done to the Public Health Service, institutions like the Rockefeller Foundation, medical research in general, and the customary life of doctors. It is not that Mr. Lewis's Jacques Loeb, Professor Gottlieb, is contained altogether in a solution of romantic tears, or that his Metchnikoff, Dr. Sondelius, is a sophomore scientist seen sophomorically. It is rather that these characters show his conception of scientific inquiry to be debased. And in Martin Arrowsmith, the details of his career, his mind and thinking and emotions, his science and the larger science it is bound to, are romantic, sentimental, and above all trivial. Himself an adolescent whose experience is never mature or complex, he is portrayed in an adolescent conception of what he stands for. As a mind Martin suffers from arrested development, as a scientist he is a fool. Mr. Lewis does indeed picture certain genuine absurdities of scientific research in the book, but never the really dangerous absurdities. And the austerity, complexity, illuminations, frustrations, methods, goals, and conditions of scientific thinking never get into the book at all. The realities of science, worthy or unworthy, the great world of science in its entirety, are altogether passed by.

Is not the same true of Mr. Lewis's characters in general? Leora Arrowsmith is emotionally undeveloped. Ann Vickers is an immature mind and her emotions are childlike. Dodsworth is so simple a personality that one doubts if he could have managed a corporation. His wife Fran, who is Lewis's most developed character, is not developed past a simple statement of frigidity, a statement which does not disclose either the content or the roots of frigidity. Maturity of mind, maturity of emotion, complexity of character or experience, profundity of aspiration, despair, achievement, or failure—they are not discoverable in these books. They are not present in America so far as these books try to be an index to America. Mr. Lewis is not at ease when he is on the side of his characters, he is at ease when he is deriding them, when they are his butts. But his attack on them consists of showing that they are without complexity, sophistication, true power, or genuine depth. Select whatever you will, love, lust, family affection, courage, meditation, fantasy, childhood, religion, socialism, education, friendship, villainy, pain—and you find it shallow. The lives explored are uncomplicated, the experience revealed is mediocre.

Again there is no point in asking whether some part of this may be a defect of the novelist, for even if any be, a greater part certainly originates in the literary fallacy. In Mr. Lewis's work a sizable portion of our literature went out to answer questions whose answers it had worked out as assumptions in advance. The rationale existed beforehand as a chart, and when literature inquired what American life was like, it knew in advance that American life would turn out to be trivial, shallow, and mediocre. It is a short step from mediocrity to contemptibility. In the mood to which Mr. Lewis brought more energy, talent, enjoyment, and even affection than anyone else, novelists for a long time conceived of fiction as an exercise in expressing the contemptibility of American life. True to the pattern of fads, fiction began to develop specific types. There was the farm novel: frustration, cretinism, bastardy, and the squalor of the soul. A current folkway of writers was to seek the good life on little farms in Connecticut, whence frustrate peasants had been driven out, but the novel of farm life as unspeakably degraded moved all across our geography till the Pacific Ocean put a boundary to it. There was the novel of Prohibition, the novel of the repressed high school teacher, the novel of the American male as an unskilled lover, the novel which daringly denounced the courthouse gang—but a more studious mind than I has made a list. An admirer of this fiction, which he called the novel of protest, once set out to name its principal themes, with no apparent knowledge that he was writing humor:

the American passion for "bigness" and success, high pressure salesmanship, shoddy commercial products, poor housing conditions in urban areas, the narrow, lethargic, platitudinous, and often hysterical mob mind, corruption in government, labor injunctions, racketeering, standardization in education, industry, and art, the deportation of radicals, the abridgment of our constitutional liberties, the contract system of prison labor, militarism, the subsidizing of large corporations, political patronage, blue laws, nationalism, the legalized extortion of big business, sweat shops in the needle trades, racial prejudice, the stretch system in factories, inelastic marriage statutes, capital punishment, the entrance of religion into politics, imperialism, profiteering, a nation half boom and half broke, jingoism, rate inflation by public utilities, law evasions, our present jury system, election frauds, bigotry, child labor, the Ku Klux Klan, and wage slavery of every kind.

Of this sort of thing criticism has lately been saying that fiction had turned from experience to data, and that is true. But such a list merely names some of the ways in which fiction was finding the Americans mediocre or contemptible. One observes an omission: the list makes no finding that literary persons are mediocre or may be considered contemptible. However, in due time Mr. Hemingway was to close that gap.

By process of critical rationale, by dedication, by fashion, by a variety of other avenues, writers have come to occupy the site chosen for them by Mr. Brooks, for which Mr. Cabell found a suggestive name, the High Place. Biography has become a study of mediocrity and contemptibility in our past, apparently to excuse us by accusing our ancestors. Like fiction and criticism, it is a withdrawal to the High Place. Some writers, following Harold Stearns's manifesto, are making a literal withdrawal. In American society there is no joy nor light nor hope, no dignity, no worth; reality cannot be found there and art cannot live. So the Artist will seek societies where art can live, finding joy and hope and beauty, experience deep in the grain, Paris, the French Riviera, Cornwall, the Mediterranean islands, Russia. What life in America abundantly lacks exists abundantly in such places. Thought is free there, art is the universal goal of human effort, writers are universally respected, and human life has a claim on the interest of literary men which in America it assuredly has not. But whether physical or only spiritual, the withdrawal to the High

Place has become an established mode of literature and this mode dominates the literature to which the generality of writers acknowledge allegiance. The dedication of the High Place may be granted easily, but the illumination of its inhabitants seems to consist of perceiving the inferiorities of their countrymen. Few writers ever spoke of themselves in print as a superior class. The assumption is implicit in the critical rationale, but it is customary to speak not of superiority but of leadership. The superiority of the caste is the inferiority of the life withdrawn from. From the High Place, the Americans are the fall guys of the world, sometimes dangerous as a mob, less often pitiful as well-meaning boobs, but most often tawdry, yokelish, acquisitive, coarse, an undifferentiated mass preyed on by mass passions and dominated by mass fears.

Turn now to Mr. Ernest Hemingway's fiction for evidence to carry us a little farther. Here are memorable portraits of racketeers, thugs, hunters of big and small game, prizefighters, bullfighters, poolroom hangers-on, prostitutes, expatriate idlers, soldiers, a miscellany of touts, sportsmen, entertainers and the like, and some millionaires and writers of whom the principal assertion is that they are sexually impotent. Mr. Hemingway's themes are death, the fear of death, the defiance of death, and the dangers to which male potency is exposed—and it is easy to see what he praises. He praises aggressiveness, courage, male wariness, male belligerence, the instinctual life, war and fighting, sexual intercourse, and a few primary loyalties immediately associated with them. It is also easy to say what life is not, as his fiction represents life. Life, so far as it can be desired or respected, does not exist above the diaphragm. It is activated by digestion, the surge of adrenalin into the bloodstream at crises of danger or defiance, and the secretion of the testicles. His hero is a pre-Piltdown stage of man, a warily aggressive anthropoid who goes down fighting. Intellectual life does not exist even in rudimentary form, except that the contempt heaped on it grants it a kind of existence. There is no social life, there is not even a society. Pithecanthropus Erectus prowls a swamp so sown with danger that the honors, constraints, bonds, prohibitions, and decencies of men living together merely add another, extreme form of danger to it. They are weaknesses of less perfect animalities who have risen to the ethical and social development of, say, Cro-Magnon man; the superior, more primitive anthropoid merely uses them to destroy him. There is hardly even love, though Mr. Hemingway has written many love stories, one of which may well be the best of his period. Piltdown man couples with his female and the physical mating is clean, but the beauty of this function is corrupted when love tries to add spiritual associations to it. They are decadent—anything is decadent which may diminish male vigor or deflect its functioning. Life has grandeur in that it may aggressively defy violent death, and it has tragedy in that the defiance may be vain.

In short, the world most of us live in and the qualities by which we try to live are unrecognized in Mr. Hemingway's fiction. True, criticism has decided that the progress of world disorder finally led him to a great affirmation, and Mr. Geismar, whom I have quoted before, seems honestly to believe that the doom of civilization was averted and hope came back to the Western world when Mr. Hemingway found a cause he could believe in. Still, it does not appear that the dying murderer of *To Have and Have Not* has altered Mr. Hemingway's basic values

when he has learned that adrenalin spurts in vain into the bloodstream of one man alone. Nor, after prayerful search, can I find that the values by which the life of men is to be judged have been altered in the novel to which Mr. Hemingway so presumptuously prefixed a quotation from John Donne. It is true that Mr. Hemingway's constant preoccupation with belligerence, cruelty, and inflicted death has contrived to associate itself with symbols in which the rest of us find values that ennoble life. But in the novel life is not ennobled by those symbols. The emphasis still suggests that though the sexual act may be very fine, the act of killing is an orgasm far surpassing it in intensity. The world for which Robert Jordan faithfully sacrifices his life appears to be, in prospect, still a swamp which men who are mere bowels and autonomic nervous systems will prowl to the same ends, though perhaps this time in bands of gangsters rather than as lonely killers. The novel is not aware, even in vision, of society as civilization or of life as something affected by the fore-brain.

From the beginning up to now, both implicitly and explicitly, with a vindictive belligerence, Mr. Hemingway has always attacked the life of the mind, the life of the spirit, and the shared social experience of mankind. Certainly he finds them contemptible; it is a legitimate guess that they scare him. The point is, however, that his disdain of intelligence, contempt of spirituality, praise of mindlessness, and adoration of instinct and blood-consciousness have many connections with other literary values held elsewhere in the general movement. They are related to the cult of pure esthetics, to the mystical cult of which D. H. Lawrence was the most gifted exponent in English, to the manias of doom that obsess Mr. Faulkner (who has much else in common with Mr. Hemingway), and to such clotted phobias as those that distinguish the work of Robinson Jeffers. If some areas of literature made a thesis of the inferiority of Americans, other areas exalted the thesis to make men inferior to the animals. It is a short step from thinking of the mob to thinking of the wolf pack, from the praise of instinct to war against reason, from art's vision of man as contemptible to dictatorship's vision of men as slaves. Such considerations, however, do not concern us. We have merely to repeat that Mr. Hemingway's fiction is separated from our common experience. By a different path he has come to the High Place. He is uncomfortable there for he finally comes to use the word "writer" as an epithet of contempt, as folklore has the wounded snake striking its fangs into its own body. But there he is and love, work, decency, achievement, aspiration, and defeat, as people know them who are neither writers nor bullfighters nor anthropoids, do not come within his awareness. Or, if they sometimes intrude on him, they only press the trigger of his scorn.

I think that we have enough clues now and may let the rest of the period's literature go undescribed, coming forthwith to the symbols which this literature agreed to accept as comprehending the whole. What this generation had to say about life, it was generally agreed, found final expression in Mr. Eliot's poem, "The Waste Land." I do not propose to add to the thousands of pages that have analyzed it, but only to mention the passage in which Tiresias, "Old man with wrinkled female breasts," is present at the tawdry seduction of the typist home at teatime by the young man carbuncular, the small house agent's clerk on whom assurance sits as a silk hat on a Bradford millionaire. Here thirty concentrated lines of verse render life in the modern world as a cheap inanity, love as a vulgar ritual without feeling or significance, and mankind as too unimportant to justify Mr. Eliot's hatred of Apeneck Sweeney.

It is a crucial passage, crucial not only in Mr. Eliot's poetry but in the literature of our time. All Mr. Eliot's other perceptions support it, down to the time when his forehead was crossed with ashes on the first day of a later Lent. In it an entire literary movement makes a final judgment. Literature looks at human beings and says that this is what their experience amounts to. It commits itself. Then, having made the commitment, Mr. Eliot went on to prophesy. He was right to do so. For if personality and experience in our time were justly rendered in this passage, then there could be little doubt that life must come out as he predicted.

This is the way the world ends
This is the way the world ends
This is the way the world ends
Not with a bang but a whimper.*

It happens that Mr. MacLeish had a moment of sharing this vision, and he envisaged the end of the world coming down upon a gaudy circus performance when "The armless ambidextrian was lighting A match between his great and second toe," and then above the white faces and dazed eyes of the audience

There in the sudden blackness the black pall
Of nothing, nothing, nothing—nothing at all.‡

Literature, I say, had committed itself.

*From *Collected Poems 1909–1935* by T. S. Eliot, copyright, 1936, by Harcourt, Brace and Company, Inc. and reprinted with their permission and with the permission of Faber and Faber (Publishers) Ltd. from *The Hollow Men,* by T. S. Eliot.

‡From "The End of the World." Reprinted by permission of Archibald MacLeish and Houghton Mifflin Company.

It had made a final judgment. It had reached the end of a road. In homelier words, it had got out on the end of a limb. So then the end of the world arrived.

Who are the people to whom Mr. Mac-Leish has been appealing so passionately —on behalf of whom he has accused writers of being as irresponsible as common criminals? They are only that audience of white faces and dazed eyes whom even judgment day could not stir to an awareness of anything at all. And when the end of the world came no whimpering was to be heard, except perhaps a literary whimpering, but the typist home at teatime and young man carbuncular decided that the world should not end. Nothing whatever changed in the typist and the house agent's clerk when the bombers came over London or the shock of Pearl Harbor traveled across this country. But war provided an appeal of judgment. The typist and the clerk had fortitude, sacrifice, fellowship; they were willing to die as an act of faith for the preservation of hope. They were hope, the soul and body of hope. They were staunchness, resolution, dedication. In fact they were incommensurable with what Mr. Eliot's poem had said they were. In "The Waste Land," I remarked, an entire literary movement made a final judgment on mankind. It committed itself. It got out on the end of a limb. But mankind turned out to be otherwise. It was not what literature had said it was. Furthermore, literature is now, temporarily at least, willing to accept the reversal of judgment. It has, temporarily at least, agreed to accept courage, fortitude, sacrifice, dedication, fellowship, willingness to die for the sake of the future—it has agreed to accept such attributes as a norm by which mankind shall be judged.

But perhaps it was the business of literature all along to take account of such attributes. It was not the typist and the young man carbuncular who were trivial. It was not their experience nor their emotions nor the realities they lived by that were trivial. It was the imagination of writers who passed judgment on them.

Return to the question I asked toward the beginning of these lectures. If one who was ignorant of American life during the 1920s, say Mr. Geismar, were to consult the books of, say, Mencken, Lewis, Hemingway, Dos Passos, and Wolfe in an effort to understand it, could he trust their description? I answered no. We have come far enough to turn that answer into an inquiry.

Consider the work of Mr. Dos Passos. No insincerity can be alleged against him, no malice, no kind of irresponsibility, especially the kind which Mr. MacLeish charges against the generation. Mr. Dos Passos has an austere conception of the responsibility of a novelist. All his fiction proceeds from a vision of life in America since the turn of the twentieth century, a vision of the time and the society as a whole. It is conceived with great power. It is worked out with a technical mastery which no contemporary has excelled. It is never suffered to depart from his vision.

One might, of course, hold that this vision is sometimes mistaken. Thus the damage done to our society by his Ward Moorehouses and Charley Andersons would indeed have been insignificant if such men had been what they seem to Mr. Dos Passos—if they had been just feeble timeservers or drunken lechers, antlike creatures carried crazily on chips by a great flood. But they were able to damage our society because that is precisely what they were not. Because Ward Moorehouse had a powerful intelligence which he employed in clearly calculated operations with effectively mastered tools. Because Charley Anderson, as a class, did not spend his time in debauchery but instead with an ascetic sobriety and an undeviating single-mindedness operated a mastered technology in his own service, toward ends which he did not in the least misconceive.

Specific inaccuracies, however, are less important for our study than the enveloping conditions in which Mr. Dos Passos's characters exist. They are always held to his vision with complete fidelity. But, ferocious as the injuries inflicted on them are, they do not move us much. These half-drugged men and women marching past milestones of indignity toward graceless deaths do not engage us to share their pain. The truth is that they hardly seem to suffer pain. Nothing theoretical or ideological is missing. Art has not failed to put any of its instruments at the service of life. Nevertheless these creatures, these integrations of behavior, are removed so far from us that they seem to be seen through a reducing glass. They lack a vital quality, they seem like automatons. It is as if, shall I say, the doom they meet is merely a literary doom.

If one sets against them the characters of the most considerable American novelist developed during the 1930's, James Farrell, one sees at once what the vital lack is. Mr. Dos Passos and Mr. Farrell conceive the function of fiction identically. But when a Farrell character is injured he bleeds, and when society wrongs one the reader is wronged with him, and this fails to happen in the Dos Passos novels. Certainly Mr. Dos Passos does not lack anger or compassion—nor the irony and pity which Mr. Hemingway found so funny when a bigger man than he praised them. But he remains on the High Place when looking at his people. His vision is afar off, from the mountain top. Whereas the monstrous cruelties inflicted on Studs Lonigan and the O'Neills, the monstrous

brutalities they are forced to commit, are indeed monstrous precisely because they are not seen from the mountain top. They are monstrous because we feel that they are an intolerable impairment of human dignity. Precisely because human life is thought of as having inherent worth, things done to men may indeed be intolerable. Precisely because the experience of men has dignity there may be tragic experience. Precisely because men are not contemptible the cruelty and injustice inflicted on them can move us to say this must not be borne.

With Mr. Farrell for illustration, however, I have come outside the decade. It is proper to consider some who in that decade stood outside the official doctrines and made the affirmation I have found in him. But first let me a little generalize what we have said so far.

We have examined a system of ideas which held that American culture was barren and American life malformed, tawdry, and venal. From this the next step, soon taken, was to find the cultural traditions actively evil and the life they expressed vile. It is easy to say that from this literature was gone a sense of the heroic in our past. It is easy to say that American literature had lost all feeling of the greatness of America, whether past or present, and of its place in the Western world and its promise to civilization. It is easy to say that belief in the future, the very feeling of hope, was gone. But to say this is superficial, for much more was gone.

Not only heroes are scarce in this literature. In books which leading writers wrote and leading critics praised, the gospel of the established church, nothing is so rare as merely decent people. Where in the literature of the 1920's is the man or woman who lived a civilized life dedicated to the mature values of civilization?

Where is the man who accepts the ordinary decencies and practises them with good will, meeting with self-respect and courage the human adventure of birth, growth, education, love, parenthood, work, and death? The man who is loyal to his friends, believes in his country, is a good citizen, loves his wife, works for his family, brings up his children, and deals resolutely with the vicissitudes, strains, anxieties, failures, and partial successes that compose our common lot? In the official Scriptures that man either does not exist at all or exists as an object of derision. Mr. Dos Passos overlooks him, he is beyond the concern of Mr. Faulkner, Mr. Hemingway says that he lacks maleness, and when Mr. Lewis abandons his amiable or occasionally dangerous fools he is unable to conceive that man above the level of a high-school boy.

Here criticism usually demurs. The final phase of finance capitalism, the cynicism of an inflationary boom, Prohibition, racketeering, the decay of politics, the Scopes trial, the Sacco–Vanzetti case, innumerable other data of the same kind — such evidence as this, we are told, appalled writers, who were right to dissociate themselves from it altogether. With an odd pride Mr. Edmund Wilson has remarked that this generation of writers attacked their culture more unanimously and more continuously than any other known to history. Even so, a vagrant mind wonders why orthodox dogma was unable to perceive in America any will to oppose these things except among literary folk. One goes on to point out, moreover, that not only decency and righteousness are gone from the people whom this literature exploits but, as well, the simple basis of humanity. And that, one decides, makes merely silly the distress which criticism tells us was behind the exploitation. If man is a predatory animal, then surely it is silly of writers to blame him when he acts according to his nature. The wolf may not be hated for wolfishness nor the boob for stupidity: the anger of literature would be idiotic. But the idea that writers might be idiotic is abhorrent and so, summing up, one turns from it to say instead that literature's dissociation from common experience, achieved by systematic logic, results in a fundamental judgment, and a false judgment, on the nature of man. . . .

Let us, however, turn from what I have called the official literature of the 1920's — the body of writing which was accepted by most writers as composing the movement, and which was conscious of itself as representing the age. Nothing about the period is more remarkable than the fact that second-rate writers were commonly less susceptible to the literary fallacy than their betters. But I propose to speak of certain first-rate writers who stood outside the movement.

To name only a few, when one comes to Carl Sandburg, E. A. Robinson, Willa Cather, Stephen Vincent Benét, and Robert Frost one enters a world quite different from that of the poets and novelists I have discussed and the critics who made out work-sheets for them. It is certainly not a world sugary or aseptic, washed clean of evil, or emptied of hate, injustice, cruelty, suffering, failure, or decay. No one in the generation has written with fiercer anger of the exploitation of men than Mr. Sandburg. No one in the generation has more witheringly rebuked the ebbing from our consciousness of certain elements of greatness in our tradition than Miss Cather or Mr. Benét. In Mr. Frost's poetry there is a resentment of indignities inflicted on men so fierce that compared to it Mr. Lewis's protest seems no more than a rowdy bellow and Mr. Hemingway's a rather craven sob. The difference is not that these writers fail in any way to be aware of evil or that any of them fail to understand the indecencies of life. It is only a difference of opinion—a difference of opinion about the dignity of man. That is all but it is a final difference, one that can never be resolved.

The poetry of Robert Frost affirms what the orthodox literature of the 1920's denies: that human experience has dignity. Human feeling has finality. Grief may be hopeless and rebellion may be futile but they are real and so they are tragic. Tragedy may be immitigable but it *is* tragedy. The integrity of experience is common to us all and is sacred in us all. Life *has* sanctity; whether fulfilled or unfulfilled, it *is* worthy, it *can* be trusted, it *has* a dignity that cannot be corrupted. The experience of men has a fundamental worth which neither other men, nor God, nor a hostile fate can destroy. Hold the poems to any light, look at any edge or angle of them, and they always come to the same focus. A worthless hired man comes back to an adopted home to die with people who know his worthlessness. A woman once mad washes her dishes beside Lake Willoughby in the knowledge of what made her mad and the knowledge that she will be mad again. A lover of forest orchids whom the acquisitive society has crippled signs a legal release, knowing exactly what it was that cut off his feet. In them all is an infrangible dignity. On that infrangible dignity of man Frost's poetry stands foursquare and in Frost's poetry American literature of our time makes its basic affirmation. Man is the measure of things. Man's experience is the measure of reality. Man's spirit is the measure of fate.

The literature we have glanced at lacks this basic acknowledgment of the dignity of man. That is why it is a trivial literature—why the Waste Land of Mr. Eliot

and the Solutrean swamp of Mr. Hemingway are less than tragedy, smaller than tragedy. Bulls and male sharks may die in agony, and perhaps there is beauty in the moment of total aggressive force going down before superior force, but though the pain they suffer may shock our nerves we cannot possibly feel their death as tragic. The diminished marionettes of Mr. Dos Passos do not move us to either pain or protest. Conceived as aggregations of reflexes, they lack the humanity which alone gives significance to suffering or cruelty. The frustration of an animal cannot be tragic. The accusation that any man is base or has done evil means nothing at all, unless baseness and evil are defections from the spirit of man. Injustice is an empty word unless man is the measure of justice. There can be no sin unless sin robs man of a state of grace.

That is why so many literary attitudes of our time led eventually to cynicism, heartbreak, or neurotic collapse. Out of them has come much penitence and much of that penitence is merely absurd. It was always possible to inquire "What art?" when someone told us long ago that a spirit bruised by the mediocrity of the life round it intended to seek healing in dedication to beauty. The same question disposes of several dozen literary confessions which have told us that the penitents found no life whatever in beauty, that the palace of art proved to be a house of the dead. Again, those who fled the culture of America, which stifled thought and forbade art and made war on freedom, were presently back from various European Utopias strangely shocked because something Utopian, something which clearly could not be charged against America, had interfered with thought and art and freedom. Another group were betrayed into a more painful bewilderment. They undertook to identify themselves with the workers of the world, only to perish of a dilemma. The blue jeans of the Noble Worker were ceremonial vestments by definition and yet, by earlier definition, the bodies they covered had been denied immortal souls. Three quarters of a literary movement died of internal friction.

Such fragile attitudes are unimportant. They merely move one to inquire whether the lack of intelligence observed was in the culture complained of or in the writers complaining. What counted was not the fragility of small attitudes but the falsity of the fundamental literary attitudes. As the catastrophe of our time moved on to its last act, it became clear that literary thinking had got caught in a steel trap of its own making. Literature now found itself summoning men to die for institutions, traditions, possibilities, and hopes which it had lately described as either nonexistent or contemptible. And the men whom it summoned to die for them were the inferior creatures who had lately been incapable even of perceiving, still more of understanding, the values which could make them consent to die.

For it is clear to you that I have been talking about something which need not necessarily be phrased in literary jargon. I have been talking about democracy, I have been talking, in fact, about a very specific form of democracy which first became a faith, first established the tenets and developed the energy of a faith, and first brought that faith to the problems of men living together in society, here in America. It is true that not many writers of the 1920's formally or even consciously opposed democracy. It is proper to remember that a few did. There were some who formally analyzed democracy as a mob of inferior men, dominated by mob lusts and mob panics and conditioned by the swinishness of the average man. Such writers opposed democracy, and so did a number of the period's least stable minds, prettily coquetting with notions of American monarchy and various other lightly literary lunacies, though of course the stampede of literary men to formidable absolutisms, whether communist or fascist, was a phenomenon of the next decade. However, the sum was small and the effect unnoticeable even in the coterie press.

Apart from these, it is just to say that the writers of the period avowed an honest respect for the word "democracy." A word is only a word, however. American democracy is not a word but American men and women, the beliefs they hold about themselves and one another, institutions they maintain to safeguard their beliefs and to fulfill their hopes, and the goals, ideals, constraints, and prohibitions they share and mutually acknowledge. It was precisely these people and these ideas, feelings, institutions, traditions, and culture which the literature of the period rejected. For these people and their culture the orthodox writers of the period had, as their books prove, an antipathy ranging from mere disillusionment or mere distaste, through hatred, to contempt. No wonder, then, that when judgment day came so incomparably otherwise than Mr. Eliot had predicted, the ideas of many literary men became schizophrenic. Ordinary man must now save the democratic way of life. But one earlier premise held that that way of life was not worth saving. And another earlier premise held that those who must save it could not save it. Either premise seemed to make it impossible to take a stand.

But this merely repeats what I have just said in other words. The Christian view of life holds that men are entitled to primary respect because they are all the children of God—"inasmuch as ye have done it unto one of the least of these my brethren ye have done it unto me." The view of life, Christian or non-Christian, which in all ages is called humanistic holds that man is entitled to primary respect because only in man's consciousness can the universe be grappled with. And the democratic view of life holds quite simply that the dignity of man is unalienable.

But respect for this unalienable dignity is precisely what had been drained from the literature of the 1920's. Mr. MacLeish's indictment of modern American literature which I began by quoting says that writers failed to safeguard our democracy between the two great wars. There can be no appeal from that judgment. But they failed to safeguard it because they failed in primary respect for democratic man and primary understanding of his experience.

I have remarked that for several years now literature has been confessing its errors. The confession of such an error as this is a confession of betrayal. It amounts to a confession that what truly was bankrupt was not American civilization but the literary way of thinking about it. That way of thinking, it is now quite clear—it is temporarily clear even to writers—was not competent to bring in trustworthy findings. It was not an adequate, an accurate, or a dependable instrument. It would not give results that could be used. The principal effort of literature has, by its own confession, failed. It has failed because of the insufficiency of its means. It has failed because a people, a culture, and a civilization cannot be held to literary values.

FREDERICK J. HOFFMAN (1909–1967) held a Ph.D. from Ohio State University and taught at the University of Oklahoma, the University of Wisconsin, and the University of California at Riverside. At the time of his death he was Professor of English at the University of Wisconsin at Milwaukee. Twentieth century American literature was his field of special interest, and his major works include *The Little Magazines* (1947), *William Faulkner* (1961), and *The Twenties* (1955). The latter explicitly disagrees with DeVoto's "waste land" appraisal of the 1920s literature. Hoffman admits that the writers of the decade "shifted their ground uncomfortably with respect to the question of their debt to society," but argues that they were searching for new solutions to the problems of art and life. To what degree did these writers forsake the conventions of contemporary society? Why did they speak so often of human absurdity?*

Frederick J. Hoffman

A Literary Renaissance

Not long after October 1929 people began to regret the 1920s to renounce the sins of a "wasted decade"; they admitted they had had a good time while "the gaudiest spree in history" had lasted, but they were ready now to assume the roles of adult, mature persons. No more pathetic reminder of the reformed playboy exists than Charlie Wales of Fitzgerald's story, "Babylon Revisited" (written in 1931). Wales returns to Paris, after an exile, to reclaim his life. He is properly humble, regretful, resolved; he has become "a new man," learned his lesson, and will his sister-in-law please restore his daughter Honoria to him? He will now be able to take care of her: sober, restrained, solvent, and anxious to identify himself with the human race, he feels that she will secure him in his new conviction. He now believes "in character"; he wants "to jump back a whole generation and trust in character again as the eternally valuable element."

Paris, the Babylon to which he has made his journey of contrition, is itself suffering a depression of the spirit. The streets are almost empty of tourists, where a few months before they had been gay and colorful. "The Poet's Cave had disappeared, but the two great mouths of the Café of Heaven and the Café of Hell still yawned—even devoured, as he watched, the meager contents of a tourist bus—a German, a Japanese, and an American couple who glanced at him with frightened eyes." Looking upon the waste, reflecting upon the pathos, Charlie Wales suddenly realizes "the meaning of the word 'dissipate'—to dissipate into thin air; to make nothing out of something."

The "waste" is both a moral and a dramatic problem. There are those who soberly endured the antics of their American contemporaries during the 1920s; now they have become their judges. But the morally correct do not enjoy their role; they have a sense not so much of wickedness resisted as of their having been cheated out of something. Marion Peters, the sister-in-law who has kept Charlie's daughter from him, "was a tall woman with worried eyes, who had once possessed a fresh American loveliness." Between the two a quiet but intense struggle develops, a struggle of two equally strong determinations, for Honoria, the prize. If he should prove that one can morally survive the 1920s, the prize is his; if not, if there is the slightest doubt of his having fully reformed, Honoria remains with the "good woman," the woman who has sacrificed her "American loveliness" so that character might return to the American personality after an absence of at least ten years. Slowly, arduously, Wales works to regain her confidence. But the stain of the 1920s is hard to remove. Two of his friends reappear from out of the past; and, though Wales tries to keep them away, to prevent their violating the temple of his humble resolve, they do just that. The 1920s cannot be put away. The ter-

rible crime of irresponsibility, which had led to the death of his wife, haunts the atonement at the very moment of forgiveness, and Wales is once more back at the beginning, without the reward he had wished for his patient efforts to redefine himself as a responsible human being:

Again the memory of these days swept over him like a nightmare—the people they had met traveling; then people who couldn't add a row of figures or speak a coherent sentence. The little man Helen had consented to dance with at the ship's party, who had insulted her ten feet from the table; the women and girls carried screaming with drink or drugs out of public places—

—The men who locked their wives out in the snow, because the snow of twenty-nine wasn't real snow. If you didn't want it to be snow, you just paid some money.

On January 2, 1950, *Life* magazine summarized the five decades of our century in one hundred pages of pictures and comment. As is usual on such occasions, the 1920s figured prominently, and there was nothing new or unexpected in the display. From Gilda Gray to Grover Whalen, the celebrities of the time were exhibited; and the brief preface reflected upon their meaning:

When the 1920s ended in the crash it became fashionable (and merciful) to forget them, and they have been buried beneath recovery, war, and a new boom. It is startling to find the old headliners still looking as chipper as they do in these pictures taken in the past few months—startling, and pleasant. They were the life of the party and everyone loves them, even though it was not a party that the nation can afford to throw again.

What distinguishes this quotation from the Luce "capsule" is the quality of its metaphor; the 1920s were a "party" that resulted in a serious hangover. We still talk about the party but are properly repentant and resolved not to have another. The same metaphor is encountered in a collection called *The Pleasures of the Jazz Age* (1948), edited by William Hoddap: "Here is a ten-year-long weekend party in which they all participated and whose hangover never really started till the stock-market crash." These people had founded "an uncharted colony of freedom—even license—for refugees from reality." In other characterizations the 1920s were called "The Era of Wonderful Nonsense," the time of the "lost generation," the "Jazz Age," the age of Freud, Ziegfeld, and Coolidge.

In a very real sense Fitzgerald, who had been in the vanguard of those establishing this image of the twenties, helped to make it a permanent view. When the decade died in the last months of 1929 Fitzgerald "tightened his belt"; and in subsequent years he wrote a series of pieces, for *Scribner's, Esquire,* and other magazines, in which he described both the pleasures and the agonies of atonement since undergone. Fitzgerald's Charlie Wales perhaps best symbolizes the crowd who "went to the party" and had to pay the check.

The "golden boom," the "gaudiest spree in history," required in 1931 "the proper expression of horror as we look back at our wasted youth." In the 1930s Fitzgerald wrote about his "wasted youth," dwelling again and again upon its glamour and its misguided energy. The pages of *Tender Is the Night* (1934) are filled with judgments delivered upon the waste, the triviality, the pathetic effort to realize what in the decade had seemed hopelessly beyond realization. The hero, Dr. Dick Diver, sacrifices his every talent, his last ounce of energy, to keep alive an illusion that has been doomed from the start. His struggle is not with the 1920s but with a complex of enemies who, in Fitzgerald's view, had made the decade what it was: easy wealth; the falsely sentimental view of life symbolized in the Rosemary Hoyt of the film *Daddy's Girl;* the inner weaknesses and tensions of its most gifted persons; above all, its indifference to human responsibility—its inability to define the terms on which men *become* responsible. In the end Diver, on his "way out," his wife gone away with another man, pauses for a final "benediction" of that "prayer-rug" of Riviera beach that had been the scene of his greatest triumphs and his most painful defeats:

"I must go," he said. As he stood up he swayed a little; he did not feel well any more— his blood raced slow. He raised his right hand and with a papal cross he blessed the beach from the high terrace.

In the quiet blasphemy of this gesture Diver dismisses the decade and himself; he had been identified with it and his talents and charm were exhausted to preserve in it a quality it had not wanted. He is through with it, and it with him.

In spite of the indifferent reception of *Tender Is the Night,* Fitzgerald's identification with the 1920s persisted. The two were indistinguishable in the public mind. A man of great talent, he had fought a losing battle with the temptations and the frivolities of the time. In loving them for their own sakes, he had forfeited his full right to judge them incisively. But Dr. Diver's final gesture is ironically a farewell to something pathetically lost when the decade ended. "Now once more the belt is tight," he said in November 1931 *(Scribner's Magazine),* "and we summon the proper expression of horror as we look back at our wasted youth."

Sometimes, though, there is a ghostly rumble among the drums, an asthmatic whisper in the trombones that swings me back into the early twenties when we drank wood alcohol and every day in every way grew better and better, and there was a first abortive shortening of the skirts, and girls all looked alike in sweater dresses, and people you didn't want to know said 'Yes, we have no bananas,' and it seemed only a question of a few years before the older people would step aside and let the world be run by those who saw things as they were—and it all seems rosy and romantic to us who were young then, because we will never feel quite so intensely about our surroundings any more.

Nevertheless the image of the twenties that remained most clearly in the public mind in 1950 was that established by Fitzgerald in 1920, exploited and all but exhausted by him in the following years, and then reassimilated in terms of a moral view of wistful regret in the 1930s.

It required more than Fitzgerald, however, to fix that impression upon the public mind. The crash of 1929 was, after all, not only a sign of moral collapse. It was a fact of economic history, and in the 1930s economic facts were also moral facts. The sturdy and persistent men of Marx watched the collapse of Wall Street with ill-concealed pleasure and began the 1930s with a determination to wipe the previous decade entirely off the record. "Social responsibility," all but absent from the American scene for ten years, according to the leftists, now became the major concern. The sad young men were welcomed back to America, on probation, and were asked to renounce their sinful past and promised reward for their assumption of doctrinal saintliness. The men who had made a pilgrimage to Moscow instead of indulging themselves in Babylon-on-the-Seine prepared themselves for the roles of moral spokesmen. A haunting sense of missed opportunities for "social good" overwhelmed the men and women of the 1930s, who looked back upon the "nation that for a decade had wanted only to be entertained." The apostles of social responsibility used the decade as a grim reminder: there but for the grace of Marx go I. The antics of the 1920s were "cute but horrible." Never had a more suitable demonstration appeared of the tragedy of social and moral dissipation. It was ideally suited to the Marxist text, which exploited it with great ease and convincing persuasion.

Mr. Roosevelt's liberals toned down the criticism a bit, but only because they wanted it to be less Marxist, more native to the grain of American social thought. The *New Republic* and the *Nation* regained their confidence and addressed themselves to the review of a tradition they thought had been lost when Sacco and Vanzetti were destroyed. The men who had begun their careers in the 1920s revised their points of view, addressing themselves eagerly and respectfully to great "social forces." John Dos Passos, whose John Andrews had risked and suffered all for art, now, in *U.S.A.*, relegated the aesthetic conscience to that corner of his trilogy called "The Camera Eye." Hemingway sought and found a social objective in the streets of Madrid, and later had his Robert Jordan defend the line that Lieutenant Henry had deserted. They were cured, or seemed to be. They came back to see what they had earlier ignored; and what they had previously seen they now ignored.

It was the leftists of the 1930s who were the first to count the cost, and they outlined the terms of payment in phrases of economic liability, which invariably had overtones of moral judgment. The early years of the *New Masses* (1926–1929) had anticipated the pattern of criticism: a pitiful waste of great talent and promise, because these people had not the slightest respect for society. They were pathetically unable to go beyond a childish "revolution" against the bad taste of their elders, ignoring in their rebellion the really disastrous sins committed by the older generation, the sins of capitalism. There was no doubt about it: the failure to understand the social economy was a consequence of the disrespect for any sensible tradition, American or Russian.

This view of the 1920s has not yet been entirely corrected or revised. In the 1940s the perspective was changed a bit, but it was just as much distorted by current moral and social urgencies. To the men who fought in World War II and survived it, the 1920s seemed either a period of amusing but stupid gaiety or a horrible and expensive example of what the "irresponsibles" could cost a nation with moral and military commitments to the world. In the 1950 reviews of the half-century provided in radio broadcasts and popular magazines, the 1920s appeared a grotesque world, remembered for sophomoric behavior and ingenious evasions of serious responsibility. The popular mind saw the decade only in the figure of the musical revue, in Hollywood's strange version of Jay Gatsby, or in the revival of Anita Loos's Lorelei.

The work of Van Wyck Brooks, Archibald MacLeish, Bernard DeVoto, and the editors of the *Saturday Review of Literature* sounded another kind of alarm. Their arguments combined a search for a creditable American past and an appeal for a sensible atomic future: according to them, the irresponsibles of the 1920s had either not known or not respected the American tradition. A simple formula was set up: personal responsibility is above all responsibility to one's neighbor, to one's group, and to the world at large. An explosion at Hiroshima, or anywhere, accelerates that sense of responsibility, should make man more vitally concerned than ever over the men who killed and the men who were killed. Isolationism of any kind was immoral. The historical event must hereafter be the constant locus of literary reference. Above all, one must respect one's America, as had Whittier and Twain and Whitman. There was no such respect in the 1920s; writers had given a distorted view of American life, mocking what was pardonable in it, ignoring what was admirable. When they dismissed H. G. Wells as a "Fabian school ma'arm," spoke condescendingly of John Dewey, and welcomed the dismal historical metaphors of Spengler, they were committed to a grievous violation of literary proprieties—a violation that could lead only to the fascism of Ezra Pound and the solemnly obedient acceptance and defense of his unhappy views.

Such a judgment of the 1920s was a complex of both leftist and liberal views; the "Marxist" condemnation, relieved of its economic emphasis, became wholly moral and wholly traditional. Perhaps we could no longer claim that the writers of the twenties were responsible for the collapse of the American economy, but we could accuse them of having failed to provide a sufficient moral "readiness" for World War II; and we could also say that they gave us no clue to the awful responsibilities of the "atomic age."

Invariably these attacks upon the decade were the product of one form or another of moral disposition and prejudice. Fitzgerald's Charlie Wales recognized only the difficulties of atonement for serious human errors; Mike Gold described the "hollow men" (1941) as guilty entirely on the grounds of their indifference to the "right" issues or the right interpretation of them; Brooks, having earlier condemned the American past for its failure to meet his moral demands, in the late 1930s and the 1940s condemned those who had thus renounced the past; DeVoto accused writers of having committed the unpardonable sin of attending to their writing, to the neglect of certain subject matters that he thought indispensable to a proper understanding of our tradition; MacLeish called his own fellow writers of the 1920s irresponsibles for similar reasons. These critics, in their emphasis on what they thought was primarily important, in their insistence upon *their* reading of human nature and of its relationship to literature, almost invariably shared the special moral dispositions of their age. . . .

None of these critics showed respect for the values of literature, only a persistent attempt to command and direct the perceptions of literary artists in terms of an "extra-literary" set of moral imperatives. This was in part due to the "emergency" in which much of this criticism was written; during World War II almost nothing mattered but a "literature of crisis," a literature that reaffirmed what Brooks called "primary" values; and they found little or none of this "primary" literature in the 1920s. Having discovered that the writers of the 1920s were "indifferent" to the causes that led to World War II, they accused them of being irresponsible: that is, of having neglected their roles as spokesmen of a culture and thus having encouraged the public to remain indifferent and irresponsible.

All these critics were able to cite texts. The flapper of Fitzgerald's novels and stories, for example, repeated endlessly and apparently without variation her gestures of tired sophistication. "'You see I think everything's terrible anyhow,'" Daisy Buchanan says in *The Great Gatsby,* "in a convinced way 'Everybody thinks so—the most advanced people. And I *know.* I've been everywhere and seen everything and done everything.'" Through Fitzgerald and his imitators, every place seemed to take on the character of an undergraduate campus, and every person either to be living on one or in the memory of his having lived there.

Another text might be found in the pose of bright cynicism affected by Ben Hecht's newspaperman, Erik Dorn. The business of bootlegging, in which fortunes were quickly made by evading the law, was a background of *The Great Gatsby* and Dos Passos' *Manhattan Transfer.* Daisy's "advanced people" also wrote and published gloomy estimates of the melancholy results of World War I for a nation that had won it. Americans were better out of the "international gamble," which had been so patently exposed by the war (Dos Passos' *One Man's Initiation* and *Three Soldiers;* Hemingway's *A Farewell to Arms*). It was best to make "a separate peace"; desertion from public affairs was the only means of salvaging private dignity (*Three Soldiers, A Farewell to Arms, In Our Time*). Since the war had proved that the men in charge could not command respect, one was left with a problem of personal adjustment, deprived of past securities (*The Sun Also Rises*).

But no real tragic insight into the nature of man was possible in a time when the war had destroyed certain necessary illusions and the march of science had served to reduce all remaining ones. Beginning with Harold Stearns' *America and the Young Intellectual* (1921) and ending with Joseph Wood Krutch's *The Modern Temper* (1929), the decade offered one "proof" after another of moral and social incapacity. Both the village and the small city were riddled by prejudice, stupidity, callousness (Sinclair Lewis's *Main Street* and *Babbitt;* Carl Van Vechten's *The Tattooed Countess*). The clergy were transparently ridiculous and ungodly (Lewis's *Elmer Gantry;* Mencken's "Americana"). Political morality and intelligence had never reached so low a level, at least not since Mark Twain's Gilded Age (Lewis's *The Man Who Knew Coolidge;* weekly editorials in the *Nation,* the *New Republic;* Walter Lippmann in *Vanity Fair*). Numerous suggestions were offered for easy solutions of the human distress. Doctor Coué performed his "miracles" on one level of human response with as much effectiveness as Doctor Freud did in another. Edith Wharton's Mrs. Manford *(Twilight Sleep)* enjoyed an almost daily change of cult and "vision"; and the middle-aged ladies of Lewis's Zenith vied with Helen Hokinson's suburbanites in their search for the very latest word from the decade's multiple heaven.

The new social symbolism included many strangely acute designations of the period of adjustment: what Malcolm Cowley described as "significant gesture" became in the eyes of Hemingway's Count Mippipopolous the "values" of the good life, for his Nick Adams the right restraint in the use of the senses, for Jake Barnes the "pure line" of the matador artist. Fitzgerald's brooding ex-Yale man, Tom Buchanan, nibbled "at the edge of stale ideas" and invoked white supremacy as a means of explaining his own boredom and tension. His more sensitive and pathetic Abe North had "a code": he was against the burning of witches. The more articulate of the expatriates believed their social behavior to be closely associated with art, even when it was concerned entirely with the destruction of art. Dada was significantly concerned with destruction—the most vulgar gesture might be

the most significant or the most effective. The aim was to invert the scale of decorum, to exalt vulgarity and explode convention. Mr. Babbitt was found daily in a thousand pieces in Montparnasse and Greenwich Village.

Of the general images the literature of the decade impressed upon us, two are especially vivid as "classical" reminders of the time: the "pathos of the adolescent" and the "unregenerate bohemian." For the first there is the evidence of many occasions. It is contained usually in a gesture, the very vagueness of which served to thrill its readers. Undoubtedly the great early success of Fitzgerald's *This Side of Paradise* was due to its appeals to the mind of the younger generation. Its most popular gesture comes in the last two pages: Amory Blaine speaks up for the new generation, endowing it with the privileges of its immaturity. This new generation, "grown up to find all Gods dead, all wars fought, all faiths in man shaken," was to be more brilliantly and more fully characterized in other texts; but no other work was able to endow it with quite the glamour of lonely defiance to be found in the novel's last lines:

He stretched out his arms to the crystalline, radiant sky. "I know myself," he cried, "but that is all."

Again, at the beginning of the decade, the moment of adolescent awareness was shown in Sherwood Anderson's *Winesburg, Ohio,* whose George Willard experiences for the first time "the sadness of sophistication":

With a little gasp he sees himself as merely a leaf blown by the wind through the streets of his village. He knows that in spite of all the stout talk of his fellows he must live and die

nostalgia for past
hope for future

in uncertainty, a thing blown by the winds, a thing destined like corn to wilt in the sun.

This shock of realization is like a birth into a new world. Cynicism has not set in, nor has a philosophy grown. The protections accorded normal experience are removed, and the young man is forced into a world he can never really understand. This insistence upon the youth of the generation, upon its perilous freedom, proved a strong incentive to those who could claim to belong to the generation; it made those who didn't qualify wish to belong as well. In its many variations, it sounded a note of individual rebellion, of a determination to work outside conventional securities: Hemingway's Nick Adams makes a "separate peace"; Dos Passos' John Andrews calmly accepts the penalties of desertion; Floyd Dell's heroes and heroines run the gamut, from Iowa to Chicago to Greenwich Village; and Lieutenant Henry speaks for them all:

That was what you did. You died. You did not know what it was about. You never had time to learn. They threw you in and told you the rules and the first time they caught you off base they killed you.

The range of experience varies, the definition achieves different shades and degrees of meaning. But the prevailing impression is that of the very young, frightened and puzzled and defeated at the start, but determined to formulate a code that both justifies and utilizes that defeat. This was part of the tone of the 1920s: a rhetorical quality quite different from the gestures made by Frank Norris's trapped superman or Theodore Dreiser's Hurstwood. It was a pathos realized too early, with neither the setting nor the incentive to give it the quality usually associated with "tragedy."

As for the attitude of the "unregenerate bohemian," it was even more roundly condemned by those who later criticized the decade, because it apparently ignored altogether what was usually recognized as "social experience." Far from being depressed by the period of his birth, the bohemian preferred to ignore it, except in satirical acknowledgment of its absurdity. The individual became an uncompromising anarchist, a radical of a kind that has almost vanished from the American scene since 1930. There were two variations of this attitude: one assumed that the aesthetic and the social conscience were the same; the other assumed there was no such thing as a social conscience, that there was no history but only persons. It was natural enough that this latter view should condemn the type of middle-class person Cummings had scornfully called the "official." Upton Sinclair proved to be the sole active survivor of progressive liberalism in the Twenties, and Cummings was almost alone in his active sponsorship of aesthetic radicalism in the thirties. To affirm the value of the non-social personality was a difficult and unpopular task after 1929; even Maxwell Bodenheim marched in proletarian parades up Fifth Avenue in the thirties. But the basic point of view stated and dramatized in *The Enormous Room* was never altered thereafter by Cummings, except in details and kinds of reference.

Throughout the twenties writers shifted their ground uncomfortably with respect to the question of their debt to society. Of this maneuvering we have abundant evidence in Joseph Freeman's *An American Testament* and in the early history of the *New Masses*. But the position taken by Cummings is a partial sign of what in the decade was thought to be a most important privilege: that of aesthetic self-determination. From this point of view, most attacks were launched, trivial or profound or both, upon the restrictions and conventions of the world. The aesthetic radical retained a free and independent mind, refusing to permit any interference with his freedom. He was flattered to think that his views might be explained "scientifically," but he rejected without qualification the basic requirements of a scientific method. More often than not the "unregenerate bohemian" rejected philosophy as such altogether, thought himself possessed of finer instincts than the "prurient philosophers" of Cummings' poem.

The unregenerate bohemian was an extreme form of what has been an important contribution to modern culture: the emphasis, the *insistence,* upon the value of personal vision. The 1920s were one of a very few times when one could be respected for having a private view of public affairs. This private view applied not only to actual headline copy but to systems of philosophical thought, to scientific discoveries, to investigations of the nature of man and his world, and to theories of the writing and value of literature.

Much of the activity thus sponsored was of course reckless and irresponsible in its neglect of logic and in its sporadic enthusiasms. Nevertheless the literary activity of the decade stressed the very defensible assumption that the artist's sensibility is a legitimate means of gaining insight and knowledge that are indispensable to our total view of a culture. Since the artists of the decade realized the importance of their gift, they gave a special quality of insight into facts often unchallenged or misunderstood by others. For one thing, they pointed, not to the gifts of science, but to its dangers. They risked being called frivolous and

ignorant, so that they might point out that science was not wholly good, that material progress may even be quite harmful, that an entirely satisfactory religious experience was all but impossible in a world that had "educated" itself beyond the need of it.

Perhaps their strongest (at any rate their loudest) activity consisted of their documentation of human absurdities. This criticism of the modern world, in spite of its frequent triviality, was both a profound and a necessary contribution to the knowledge we must have of our society. We realize now that for the most part it was correct and shrewd. Its value can be seen in several ways. One is its treatment of history, the act of taking the straight line of liberal prophecy and twisting it—rejecting the linear view of H. G. Wells for the cyclical view of Spengler. Another is the valuable distinction often drawn between scientific data and aesthetic—which suggested that mere science omitted much from what Ransom called "the world's body," and warned that a too narrow concern with abstract principle is almost as bad for life as it is for art. Again, this generation of critics described what they called a loss of taste in contemporary life. Vulgarity was clearly defined as a frantic and amoral desire to accumulate and to own goods; further, as the feeling that taste might be bought and did not need to be a responsible part of experience as a whole. The absurdities of the bourgeois mind and soul, the deformities of its architecture and its conscience, were never so fully documented. Perhaps the most valuable criticisms of the decade, and the most profound, were those which made it clear that defections of taste were not merely surface phenomena but betrayed an underlying inadequacy in our tradition and our culture. These criticisms could not, after all, have remained effective had they pointed merely to superficial issues. The 1920s could make no more important contribution than is contained in their most jealously guarded thesis: that history and society are and remain abstractions until they are associated with personal experience. As Arthur Mizener has said (*Kenyon Review,* Winter 1950):

. . . the situation, the moment in history, is not in itself tragic; it only provides the occasion on which the aware individual suffers the experience of unavoidable moral choices. No matter what the occasion, there is no tragedy where the forces of circumstance are not transmuted into personal experience.

If the twenties in America can be condemned seriously for a fault, it is not for their vulgarity (there is vulgarity of some sort in any time) or for their immorality (immorality in any period is ordinarily a characteristic of the move toward moral redefinition). The greatest fault was their naïveté. Men and women were often quite literally and self-avowedly ignorant of tradition. They had chosen to be; they had rejected both sound and unsound generalities and thought. As a result they were open to every new influence that came along; in most cases there was no intellectual experience to use as a measure of validity. That is undoubtedly the reason so much of the discussion of ideas in the decade seemed the talk of an undergraduate newly and overly impressed by his introductory course in philosophy.

Perhaps the young men and women of the 1950s are immensely more sophisticated, learned, and disingenuous. The theories of Freud have been greatly extended, and the attitude toward them lacks the naïve enthusiasm of an earlier generation. The French masters of literature are now not only thoroughly known; they are being revaluated and their influence upon a handful of American poets now seems a part of ancient literary history. The mood in which bulletins from Moscow were received in the offices of the *Liberator* now seems incredibly naïve. Marxism has not only undergone numerous shifts in interpretation; there have been great changes of heart regarding the "crusade that failed." It is no longer possible to imagine (one no longer has the naïve expectancy to await) a doctrine's role in saving the world. The new generation is much wiser, much less likely to be taken in—one may say, less *capable* of being taken in. But in a very real sense the assertions so often made in the twenties now seem more sensible than they did in their own time. Certainly in our own postwar world we now are convinced (and not especially shocked to find) that evil actually does exist. We are aware of the peculiar failures of scientific research and suspicious of its direct application to human affairs.

It is perhaps unfortunate that we know so much and are so helpless at the same time. In looking back upon the 1920s perhaps we ought not to be worried about the "party we cannot afford to throw again," but rather about our loss of confidence in free, if erratic, inquiry, which we seem to have abandoned along with our naïveté. Our knowledge seems to lack the strength of will that accompanied the ignorance and the errantry of the 1920s. We become more sophisticated and more inflexible with each passing year. We are competent scholars, writers, thinkers, voters; we are properly shocked when one of our fellows commits an especially noticeable error against good taste and good manners. Why, then, are we restless, uncertain, and unhappy? Why is our literature not first-rate? Why are the majority of our critical essays written about the literature of the 1920s and not about that of our own time? Something must be true of that decade that has nothing to do with the big party they were supposed to have had. Perhaps they were more sane, less frivolous, than we have been led to believe.

The most intelligent and the most sensible attitude we can have toward the 1920s, as well as toward our own time, is to accept the saving grace of an irony directed at both. They are, both of them, times of war and of the effects of war. In neither time is it possible unqualifiedly to admire or simply to repudiate man's responsibility for what has happened. That irony is expressed with an especial relevance in Allen Tate's "Ode to Our Young Pro-Consuls of the Air" (1943). . . . The times, the poet says, have once more come round to war; and each citizen is again called upon "to take/ His modest stake." We have responded to the call with full partiotism and with angry mechanical force. Once again humanity is simply divided into friend and foe; the enemy is "The puny Japanese" and "the German toad." Observing these demonstrations of moral and military might, the poet reflects upon what he

had done (or might have done) to prevent these "enemies of mind" from resuming their quarrel. . . .

The irony is addressed primarily to those who accused the writers of the 1920s of "the literary fallacy"—the critics who have been guilty of a larger "moral fallacy." For, as the poem suggests, literature is not maneuverable; a culture cannot be one thing at one time and its opposite immediately thereafter. An extreme neurosis of "social conscience" has led the judges of the 1920s into a trap of false criticism; it has assumed that the literature produced in the decade was cynically or irresponsibly (and thus dishonestly) engaged in corrupting an entire nation. These judgments suffer from a serious loss of perspective. The critics who made them have chosen to make what they need (what they will) out of the 1920s. They have insisted that literature should serve a moral objective of an extraordinarily narrow and limited kind. Since it has not seemed to do so, they have condemned it for not meeting their terms. This is not the way to a just or accurate estimate; it is a victim of its own narrowness of vision, and it cannot or should not endure beyond the limits of its occasion.

After attending Oberlin College BRUCE CATTON (b. 1899) became a newspaper reporter, a Washington correspondent, and in 1948 a special assistant to the Secretary of Commerce. In recent years he has devoted himself to writing and editing, in 1954 winning both the Pulitzer Prize for history and the National Book Award. His books on the Civil War are held in high esteem by historians and the reading public alike. He became senior editor of *American Heritage* magazine in 1959 and in that capacity wrote the introduction to the magazine's special issue on the Twenties (1965). Catton sees the decade as "full of restless vitality." He maintains that most of the "tag lines" applied to these years are wrong, although he recognizes much of the surface fantasy. To what extent does Catton temper Frederick Lewis Allen's view of the period? Why does Catton feel that the key to the Twenties lies in the decade's transitional character?*

Bruce Catton

A Restless Generation

The decade of the nineteen twenties was at one and the same time the gaudiest, the saddest, and the most misinterpreted era in modern American history.

It was gaudy because it was full of restless vitality burgeoning in a field where all of the old rules seemed to be gone, and it was sad because it was an empty place between two eras, with old familiar certainties and hopes drifting off like mist and new ones not yet formulated. It was misunderstood because so many of its popular interpreters became so fascinated by the things that floated about on the froth that they could not see anything else.

Most of the tag lines that have been attached to it are wrong. It was, we are as-sured, the period when *everybody* did fantastic things. Everybody detested Prohibition, patronized bootleggers, made atrocious gin in the bathtub and worse beer in the basement, and, inspired by the products of these activities, danced the Charleston. Everybody bought stocks on margin or Florida lots on binder clauses and confidently expected to become rich before old age set in. Everybody put his moral standards away in moth balls, so that neither the scandalous doings in Washington nor the murderous forays of the Chicago gangsters seemed very disturbing. Everybody, in short, was off on a prolonged spree, and the characteristic figure of the era was the Flapper, the girl who bobbed her hair and wore short skirts

*© Copyright 1965 by American Heritage Publishing Co., Inc. Reprinted by permission from *American Heritage* Magazine, August 1965.

with nothing in particular beneath them and put in her time piling in and out of open cars populated by collegians in coonskin coats.

It makes an entertaining picture—it made one at the time, in a way, for the people who were in it—but it is at best only a partial picture.

The first thing to remember is that the word "everybody" is much too inclusive. There were a great many people in the United States in the nineteen twenties, and most of them were serious, hard-working people who did their best to earn a living, bring up their children, live decently by the best light they had, and lay away a few dollars for their old age. Most of them never saw the inside of a speakeasy, most never really tried to make gin or beer at home, and anyone over the age of twenty-six who danced the Charleston regretted it immediately—it was an exercise in all-out acrobatics rather than a dance, and only the young could manage it. Acceptance of the Prohibition law was so widespread that repeal of the Eighteenth Amendment was not voted, or ever seriously considered, until after the decade had ended. Certainly the vast majority bought neither stocks, bonds, nor Florida real estate and never had the faintest notion that with a little luck they could soon stroll down Easy Street. They were just as deeply disturbed by Teapot Dome and Al Capone as anyone would be today, and if these and other phenomena helped to destroy confidence in public leadership, it ought to be added that the kind of leadership that was given to the American people in those years was pretty poor.

Nevertheless, the decade did have its own peculiar character—because it was a time of unending change.

It was a hollow time between wars. The 1914–18 war, which had been ever so much more cataclysmic than anybody had imagined any war could be, was over, but it had left smouldering wreckage all over the landscape; and if the next war was not yet visible, there was ominous heat lightning all along the horizon to warn that there had been no real break in the weather. The certainties the adult American was used to, in 1920—the basic assumptions about world society which he had always taken for granted—were obviously either gone forever or rapidly going. Europe, which had always seemed to be the very center of stability, had collapsed. Of the great empires which had maintained order and set standards, some had vanished without trace and the survivors were mortally injured; Europe was a center of disorder, with monstrous doctrines either being followed or vigorously preached; and the one certainty was that things would get worse before they ever got better.

There was an immense, all-pervading disillusionment. The nation's highest ideals had been appealed to during the war, so that to win the war seemed the holiest of causes; the war had been won, but it was hard to see that anything worth winning had been gained; the idealism had been used up, and people had an uneasy feeling that they had been had. The Prohibition act contributed to the letdown. Here was a social experiment which, as President Herbert Hoover correctly said, had been adopted with the noblest of motives, but nothing was working out as had been anticipated, and the problems the law was supposed to solve seemed to have been made worse; the majority was not yet ready to discard the law, but it was beginning to see that something somewhere was awfully wrong with it.

So lots of people became materialists.

The light of faith was flickering low; the average citizen had his own, private faith in the relationship between himself and his Maker, but his faith in the world itself and in the values on which it operated was not robust. It was easier, indeed it was almost necessary, to center one's attention on the material things that were going on in this country.

A great deal was going on, and it was immensely stimulating. The world was in the act of shifting gears—not without grating—starting to move with bewildering speed, and if the destination was wholly unclear, the speed itself was exhilarating.

The age of the automobile was arriving. In 1920 the average American did not own an automobile and did not suppose that he ever would; by 1930 the automobile was a necessity of daily life, and the incalculable change it was going to inflict on America—change for city, town, and countryside, for ways of living and habits of thought—was already visible. At the same time the era of mass production was coming into full effect, and mankind (most especially in America) was beginning to lay its hands on the fabulous capacity to solve any problem on earth so long as the problem was purely material. This of course was most unsettling, because it brought with it the uneasy awareness that the real problem was going to be man himself and not his ability to reshape his environment, and no one was ready to tell people what they ought to do about themselves. But it was a miraculous age. The instruments, skills, and techniques—airplanes, electronics, automation—that would change the world forever were appearing. Albert Einstein, who was known to the few Americans who had ever heard of him as an oddball professor type who thought that space was curved, had already published the for-mula that was to lead to the atomic age.

It was an exciting decade; in many ways a good time to be alive. If the spirit of the nineteen twenties took on a materialistic cast, nobody can be blamed. It was good simply to look at the surface and enjoy it.

The surface contained elements of sheer fantasy. Along with everything else, the age of mass communications was here, in exuberant, uninhibited blossoming, and the public ear could be reached as never before. In some ways those were the years of the sportswriter, the press agent, and the newspaper columnist—not the purveyor of gossip, but the man who found amusement and a large audience by discussing the items that floated about on the froth. It was the time of the big headline and the loud-speaker, which were reserved for the purely spectacular.

So the most famous people in America were a strange assortment—movie stars, gangsters, Channel swimmers, professional athletes, imaginative amateur murderers, and eccentrics of high and low degree. Before 1920, moving-picture actors and actresses were outsiders; now they were at the top of the ladder, living in the limelight as no one ever did before or since. Before 1920 prize fighting had been disreputable, outlawed in most states, tolerated in a few; now the heavyweight champion was a hero, an ideal for American youth, a man whose performances could command a box-office sale of a million dollars or more. Once in the mid-Twenties the author of a quiz program played a sly trick: by posing two innocent questions he showed that although every adult American could name and identify the star halfback at the University of Illinois, no one outside of the academic profession knew the name of that university's president.

As Westbrook Pegler said, this was the Era of Wonderful Nonsense. Publicity was the thing, and it had no standards of value except pure sensation. An American girl swam the English Channel, nonstop; the mayor of Chicago ran for re-election with the promise that he would hit the King of England on the nose if chance allowed; the President of the United States, asked how such nations as England and France could ever repay their enormous war debts without coming to utter ruin, replied drily: "They hired the money, didn't they?" A countrywoman who tended pigs was carried into court on a stretcher to testify in an earthshaking murder trial, and for a few days everybody in the country (well, a lot of people, if not quite everybody) was talking about the Pig Woman . . . and all of these things were of equal weight, they made the headlines for a few days, and then life went on as before.

Stock prices went up and up, Florida real-estate prices did likewise; supposedly realistic analysts said that this was only natural because "everybody" was in the market, and the happy theory that everybody in the United States had plenty of money overlooked the fact that farmers and wage earners were being caught in a terrible squeeze in which their bitterest protests went unheeded. A conservative senator announced that congressmen who protested about this situation were simply "sons of the wild jackass" whose cries need not be noticed, and one of the country's best-known economists said that inflated stock prices need worry no one because the nation had reached a new, permanently high plateau in which all of the old standards could be ignored.

If all of this was exciting it was not really satisfying, and people knew it. They were hungry for something they were not getting—an appeal to idealism,

to the belief that the greatest values cannot be expressed in cash or set forth in headlines. The amazing response to Charles A. Lindbergh's flight proves the point.

Lindbergh flew from New York to Paris in 1927. The Atlantic had been flown before, it was obviously going to be flown again—two or three highly publicized expeditions were poised at New York, getting ready, while the nation waited—but what he did seemed like nothing anyone had ever imagined before. He was young, boyish, unspoiled, the kind of youth people had stopped believing in, a young man nobody had heard of before, and he came to New York, waited for a good weather report, and then took off, unaided by any of the elaborate devices that would make such a flight routine nowadays. When he landed in Paris it seemed as if mankind had somehow triumphed over something that greatly needed to be beaten. After he had vanished into the over-ocean midnight, and before any word of him had come back, people waited in an agony of suspense, and when it was announced that he had indeed landed in Paris, unharmed and on schedule, there was literally rejoicing in the streets.

It was odd, and revealing. After years in which it seemed as if everybody who got any kind of fame was on the make, here was a young man who apparently had done something great for nothing. Lindbergh became the hero of the decade. We have not felt quite that way about anybody since; he lifted up the heart, and all of a sudden it was possible to believe in something once more. The response to what he did was a perfect symbol of what everybody had been lacking.

It seemed like a miracle . . . but at last the glitter faded, and like everything else, this bright deed was buried under a spate of words. There were too many words in those years. Everybody listened, and nobody got much out of it. Much of the talk came from men who were not qualified to address a large audience. At the beginning of the decade, radio had been nothing much more than a useful device by which a sinking ship could call for help; in a very few years it was central to the mass-communications business, and the man who spoke into the microphone was suddenly a power in the land. E. B. White summed it up by remarking that man's "words leap across rivers and mountains, but his thoughts are still only six inches long."

It was a time for long thoughts, but long thoughts were not often being thought, and when they were it was hard to find an audience for them. The world was passing across one of the significant watersheds in human history and the crest of the pass seemed to be situated right in the United States, but it was hard to think about anything except that, for the moment, the path led upward. The people of the nineteen twenties really behaved about the way the people of all other decades have behaved. They did a great deal of hard work, doing some of it extraordinarily well, when you stop to think about it; they carried their own individual loads of worry and aspiration and frustration along with them; and if they did some foolish things, they precisely resembled, in the doing of them, both their ancestors and their descendants.

Yet the essential point about the Twenties, the thing that makes us think of the decade as a separate era, was its curious transitional character, which was not like anything ever seen before — or since. The Twenties were years that no one who lived through them can ever forget, and they were also a time nobody in his senses would care to repeat, but you do have to say one thing for them: when the great catastrophe came, one decade after the Twenties had ended, the generation the Twenties had raised proved to be strong enough to stand the shock.

WILLIAM E. LEUCHTENBURG (b. 1922) received his
Ph.D. from Columbia University and has taught at
New York University, Smith College, and Harvard.
He is now Professor of History at Columbia,
specializing in recent American history. His book
Franklin D. Roosevelt and the New Deal (1963) won
both the Francis Parkman prize and the Bancroft prize,
while *The Perils of Prosperity, 1914–1932* (1958) is
widely used in college history courses. Leuchtenburg
holds that "the events of half a century finally caught
up with Americans" in the Twenties. Specifically the
city gained predominance over the country. Why did
this shift place such heavy strains on American society?
Why were the 1920s so militantly condemned as a time
of irresponsibility and immaturity by public spokesmen
during the depression?*

William E. Leuchtenburg

A Paradoxical Generation

Never was a decade snuffed out so
quickly as the 1920's. The stock market
crash was taken as a judgment pronounced on the whole era, and, in the
grim days of the depression, the 1920's
were condemned as a time of irresponsibility and immaturity. "It was an easy,
quick, adventurous age, good to be young
in," wrote Malcolm Cowley, "and yet on
coming out of it one felt a sense of re-
lief, as on coming out of a room too full
of talk and people into the sunlight of
the winter streets."

Time was ruthless to the heroes of the
decade. In 1929, with horrible appro-
priateness, Zelda Fitzgerald suffered a
mental breakdown. Scott Fitzgerald aged
like Dorian Gray; he wrote excellent
work which, in the serious-minded

thirties, was dismissed as trivia. Fitzgerald
himself entered that "dark night of the
soul" where it was "always three o'clock
in the morning." The insouciant Jimmy
Walker continued to make the rounds
of New York nightclubs, but in the depression days his antics no longer amused,
and he was driven from office. Mencken,
who had been the savant of the college
generation of the twenties, was brushed
aside by the college generation of the
thirties, if they read him at all, as an anti-
quated reactionary.

In 1933 the nation repealed the prohibition amendment, and with it went
the world of the speakeasy; that same
year, Texas Guinan died. Sound movies
ended the careers of many of the silent
stars. Clara Bow, who recalled halcyon

*From William E. Leuchtenburg, *The Perils of Prosperity, 1914–1932* (Chicago: The University of Chicago, 1958), pp. 269–273. © 1958 by The University of Chicago. Reprinted by permission.

days—"I'd whiz down Sunset Boulevard in my open Kissel (flaming red, of course) with seven red dogs to match my hair"— entered a sanitarium. The sound track revealed that the screen's greatest lover, John Gilbert, who had been co-starred with Greta Garbo in 1929, had a high-pitched voice. When his contract was not renewed, Gilbert committed suicide. In 1931 the Ziegfield Follies opened for the last time. In 1932, bankrupted by the depression, Florenz Ziegfield died. In the spring of 1932 vaudeville went to the grave when the Palace gave its last all-vaudeville bill. The law caught up with Al Capone in 1931, and he was sentenced to eleven years in prison for federal income tax evasion. The underworld caught up with Dutch Schultz and riddled him with bullets in a Newark barroom; dying, he uttered the baffling metrical sentence: "A boy has never wept, nor dashed a thousand kim." Dempsey's defeat, Gene Tunney's retirement, and the death of Tex Rickard brought the golden age of boxing to an end in 1929. In 1934 Babe Ruth, a pathetic waddling figure, tightly corseted, a cruel lampoon of his former greatness, took off his Yankee uniform for the last time.

The depression years killed off the symbols of simplicity the 1920s had cherished. In January, 1933—eight weeks before Franklin Roosevelt took office— Calvin Coolidge died. Henry Ford, the folk hero of the Coolidge era, was damned in the 1930's as a tyrannical employer. When he instituted the five-dollar day, he had been honored as the laboring man's warmest friend. In the depression days, Ford was hard put to defend the actions of his private police headed by a former prize fighter, Harry Bennett, a mean-tempered man with close friends in the Detroit underworld. Charles A. Lindbergh, the tousled blond airman whose flight to Paris in 1927 made him America's golden boy, suffered the trials of Job in the 1930's. On the night of March 1, 1932, his twenty-month-old son was kidnapped from his home. Seventy-two days later, the child's body was found in a patch of woods. Cruelly badgered by the press and exploited by publicity-seekers, Lindbergh and his family abandoned America for Europe in December, 1935. The magnificent Lone Eagle of the 1920's, Lindbergh, by 1940, was detested as an associate of Nazis and an avowed racist.

Throughout the 1920's, demure Mary Pickford had remained the curly-locked Pollyanna of prewar American innocence. She refused to play "bad girl" roles. Rebelling against the fashions of the time, she refused to cut her hair. In 1927, she wrote: "Sometimes it is a dreadful nightmare, when I feel the cold shears at the back of my neck, and see my curls fall one by one at my feet, useless, lifeless things to be packed away in tissue paper with other outworn treasures." In the first year of the depression, her curls were shorn, and she appeared on the screen portraying bad women.

In the 1920's the events of half a century finally caught up with America. Ever since the Civil War the United States had been industrializing at an astonishing rate—erecting great factories, filling up the empty spaces of the West, expanding its cities to gargantuan size. In the years after World War I the productive capacity of the American economy suddenly exploded at the very same time that, in large part because of the growth in productivity, the United States became the greatest of the world powers, and the city overtook the country in the race for dominance. All the institutions of American society buckled under the strain.

It was a time of paradoxes: an age of

conformity and of liberation, of the persistence of rural values and the triumph of the city, of isolationism and new internationalist ventures, of laissez faire but also of government intervention, of competition and of merger, of despair and of joyous abandon. Many of the apparent paradoxes can be explained by the reluctance of the American people to accept the changes that were occurring and by their attempt to hold on to older ways of thought and action at the same time that they were, often against their will, committed to new ones. The very men who were taken as symbols of the old order were the ones who undermined it—the Victorian statesman Woodrow Wilson, who presided over the transition to a strong state and the breakdown of isolation; the antiquarian Henry Ford, who disrupted the nineteenth-century world with revolutionary industrial technology; even Herbert Hoover, whose triumph in 1928 over Smith appeared to be a rejection of urban mores, but who himself was the unwitting architect of a new era.

The 1920's, despite rhetoric to the contrary, marked the end of nineteenth-century liberalism. In the same week in October, 1922, Lloyd George paid his last official visit as Prime Minister to the King and Mussolini marched on Rome. Although Republican ideologues like Hoover sounded the praises of laissez faire and business-minded administrators like Andrew Mellon attempted to diminish the role of government, the state continued relentlessly to augment its power. Both the civil and military functions of the federal government doubled between 1915 and 1930.

The 1920's have been dismissed as a time of immaturity, the years when America was hell-bent on the "gaudiest spree in history." But there was a great deal more to the era than raccoon coats and bathtub gin. "The world broke in two in 1922 or thereabouts," wrote Willa Cather. The year may not be accurate, but the observation is. The United States had to come to terms with a strong state, the dominance of the metropolis, secularization and the breakdown of religious sanctions, the loss of authority of the family, industrial concentration, international power politics, and mass culture. The country dodged some of these problems, resorted to violence to eliminate others, and, for still others, found partial answers. The United States in the period from 1914 to 1932 fell far short of working out viable solutions to the problems created by the painful transition from nineteenth-century to modern America. But it is, at the very least, charitable to remember that the country has not solved these problems yet.

RODERICK W. NASH (b. 1939) is Associate Professor of History at the University of Santa Barbara. He received his Ph.D. from the University of Wisconsin and is particularly interested in the social and intellectual history of the United States. Among his books are *Wilderness and the American Mind* (1967) and *The Nervous Generation: American Thought, 1917–1930* (1970). He sees the Twenties as a "time of heightened anxiety," when Americans were "groping for what certainty they could find." He feels that much of American life remained conservative, as many clung to the security of traditional attitudes and customs. How does Nash moderate the "roaring Twenties" view? How does he regard the "lost generation"? To what degree does he find life in the 1920s a continuation of patterns rooted in the nineteenth century?*

Roderick W. Nash

A Nervous Generation

Next to names like F. Scott Fitzgerald, Ernest Hemingway, and Henry L. Mencken, those of Gene Stratton-Porter, Zane Grey, and Harold Bell Wright have stirred little interest among historians of American thought and culture in the period between World War I and the Depression. Yet during these years books by the latter three appeared sixteen times on the national lists of best-sellers, while the works of the first three never appeared at all. Grey's westerns were among the top ten works of fiction every year from 1917 to 1924. Twice they were number one; twice number three. But even Grey may have been outsold in the postwar decade by an author who was not even taken seriously by the custodians of the rankings—Edgar Rice Burroughs, of the Tarzan sagas. Fitzgerald, by contrast, never ranked among the best-selling American authors of the 1920s; *This Side of Paradise* (1920) only found some fifty thousand buyers in the first few years after its publication, while the sale of Wright's *The Re-Creation of Brian Kent* (1920) approached a million copies. Mencken's appeal was highly esoteric while Hemingway's name did not make the top ten until 1940. Grey, Stratton-Porter, Wright, and Burroughs, moreover, conveyed an old-fashioned message quite at odds with that of the big names. These discoveries prompted a series of questions about American thought in the 1920s that led to the book at hand.

*From Roderick W. Nash, *The Nervous Generation: American Thought, 1917–1930*, Copyright © 1970 by Rand McNally and Company, Chicago, pp. 1–4. Reprinted by permission.

With few exceptions the general public and scholars alike have been captured and captivated by the "lost generation—roaring twenties" image of the twenties. American intellectuals supposedly emerged from the war years cynical and alienated. Rebellion became a way of life: they drifted, valueless, from bar to bar and bedroom to bedroom, members of the lost generation. Popular thought in the 1920s has also been subject to extensive mythologizing. We have been led to believe that this was the "jazz age," as F. Scott Fitzgerald labeled it in 1922, during which Americans either indulged in an orgy of irresponsible dissipation or pursued the main chance with a narrow concentration that permitted neither ethics nor altruism. It was a decade-long house party. Iconoclasm was the order of the day. Tradition and convention were so much cumbersome rubbish. The war had exposed the hollowness of the past, and the twenties turned against it savagely. So the portrait is usually painted.

While too much has been made of World War I as an influence on American thought, the spectacle of war and the frustrations of the peace did leave many citizens bewildered and shaken. But the logic that proceeds from this point to brand the twenties as a time of cynicism and rebellion, verging on nihilism, is questionable. Bewilderment and insecurity are not acceptable conditions for most persons. When one is lost, he seeks, desperately, to be found—or to find himself. The same might be said of a society. The decade after the war was a time of heightened anxiety when intellectual guideposts were sorely needed and diligently sought. Many clung tightly to the familiar moorings of traditional custom and value. Others actively sought new ways of understanding and ordering their existence. Americans from 1917 to 1930

constituted a *nervous* generation, groping for what certainty they could find. The conception of this time as one of resigned cynicism and happy reveling leaves too much American thought and action unexplained to be satisfactory.

An incomplete understanding of a small group of literati has shaped the understanding of American intellectual history in the 1920s. Intellectuals were by no means unanimous in professing the disillusionment of the expatriates, bohemians, and satirists, and even the degree to which *they* expressed it is moot. For a great many thoughtful Americans World War I did not mean intellectual derailment. The threads of continuity in the history of ideas are visible across the war years, as they are across most so-called watersheds. Henry May's *The End of American Innocence* (1959) and Morton White's conception of a "revolt against formalism" notwithstanding, prewar ideas and ideals continued into the twenties with scarcely a hitch. Indeed the war and the resulting nervousness prompted large numbers of Americans to give even stronger affirmation to values that had allegedly ended by 1920.

Some intellectuals, to be sure, redefined the nature of value. The change, however, has been represented as greater than it actually was. While criticizing the method of the absolutists and the genteel tradition, the relativists preserved much of the content of the older creed.

At the fringe of the American intellectual community stood a few really shaken minds for whom neither the old absolutism nor the new relativism and scientism sufficed as a basis for belief. Yet even these disillusioned few refused to exist with no values at all. Instead they began the American exploration of a point of view later labeled *existentialism*. Axiomatic to this position was confrontation with human futility and the absurdity of life. For this reason these intellectuals' conception of themselves as a lost generation was essential. Such a pose was part of a deliberate artistic experiment, an attempt not to deny value but rather to create from their own frustrated lives existential situations in which radically new values could be formulated. Despair and disillusion were dramatized in order to accentuate the achievement of confronting reality. Ernest Hemingway, F. Scott Fitzgerald, Joseph Wood Krutch, and the malcontented minority they represented were lost only by traditional standards. In their own terms they were finding new ways of defining and keeping a new faith.

As for popular thought in the 1920s, there has likewise been overemphasis on the revolutionary and bizarre. We have read (and with the aid of records, television, and motion pictures, heard and seen) so much about the flapper, the boot legger, and the jazz band that our conception of the era is greatly distorted. The 1920s were more than these things, just as the 1960s have been more than the jet set, hippies, and *Playboy*. We have forgotten F. Scott Fitzgerald's 1931 admonition that the jazz age concept he coined applied only to the "upper tenth of [the] nation." Perhaps even this was generous. The point is that evidence for generalizing about the mood of the decade is frequently incomplete, often by design. The twenties has been given little chance except to roar.

In fact, popular thought in these years was remarkably conservative. Beneath the eye-catching outward iconoclasm, the symbolic revolt, was a thick layer of respect for time-honored American ways, means, and rationales. The same nervousness that induced intellectuals to search for certainty prompted the general public to cling to familiar ideas with nearly hysterical intensity. It is difficult to square the popular taste of the 1920s in heroes, literature, religion, and politics, for instance, with the stereotype of the jazz age.

Suggested Readings

A fundamental prelude to understanding the intellectual mood of the 1920s is Henry F. May, *The End of American Innocence: A Study of the First Years of Our Own Time, 1912–1917* (New York, 1959), which masterfully analyzes the rebel forces that crystallized in the United States before the country's entry into World War I. May's "Shifting Perspectives on the 1920's," *Mississippi Valley Historical Review,* XLIII (December, 1956), is an invaluable interpretation. Noteworthy historiographical studies are Don S. Kirschner, "Conflicts and Politics in the 1920's: Historiography and Prospects," *Mid-America,* XLVIII (October, 1966), 219–233, and Burl Noggle, "The Twenties: A New Historiographical Frontier," *Journal of American History,* LIII (September, 1966), 299–314. The student planning serious exploration of the decade will find John D. Hicks, "Research Opportunities in the 1920's," *Historian,* XXV (November, 1962), 1–13, particularly useful.

A significant pioneer study of the 1920s is Harold E. Stearns, ed., *Civilization in the United States: An Inquiry by Thirty Americans* (New York, 1922), and Robert S. and Helen M. Lynd, *Middletown: A Study in Contemporary American Culture* (New York, 1929), a sociological examination of Muncie, Indiana, remains a classic. One of the early journalistic accounts of the decade is Mark Sullivan, *Our Times,* VI (New York, 1935), while Preston W. Slosson, *The Great Crusade and After, 1914–1928* (New York, 1931), is among the first treatments by a professional historian. Charles Merz, *The Great American Bandwagon* (New York, 1928), presents interesting glimpses into the period which add up to a whole that is greater than its parts.

Of the more recent surveys of the decade

Paul Carter, *The Twenties in America* (New York, 1968), is brief, but stimulating, and George E. Mowry, ed., *The Twenties: Fords, Flappers, and Fanatics* (Englewood Cliffs, N.J., 1963), is an admirable collection of primary sources with a short introduction that poses a number of pertinent questions. John D. Hicks, *Republican Ascendancy* (New York, 1960), adds up to a factual synthesis, occasionally touching on social and cultural matters, whereas Elizabeth Stevenson, *Babbitts and Bohemians: The American 1920's* (New York, 1967), is at times interesting, but generally superficial. Archibald MacLeish, "There Was Something about the Twenties," *Saturday Review,* XLIX (December 31, 1966), 10–13, is worth consulting, and John Braeman, Robert H. Bremner, and David Brody, eds., *Change and Continuity in Twentieth-Century America: The 1920's* (Columbus, Ohio, 1968) is excellent. For a Frenchman's appraisal of the decade, see André Siegfried, *America Comes of Age* (New York, 1927).

General intellectual histories of the United States that contain insights into the 1920s are: Merle Curti, *The Growth of American Thought* (New York, 1943), Herbert W. Schneider, *A History of American Philosophy* (New York, 1963), Stow Persons, *American Minds* (New York, 1958), Ralph Henry Gabriel, *The Course of American Democratic Thought* (New York, 1940), Henry Steele Commager, *The American Mind; An Interpretation of American Thought and Character since the 1880's* (New Haven, Conn., 1950), Oscar Cargill, *Intellectual America: The March of Ideas* (New York, 1941), Morton G. White, *Social Thought in America: The Revolt Against Formalism* (New York, 1949), Russel B. Nye, *This Almost Chosen People:*

Essays on the History of American Ideas (East Lansing, Mich., 1966), and David Van Tassel, ed., *American Thought in the Twentieth Century* (New York, 1967).

Charles Merz, *The Dry Decade* (rev. ed., Seattle, 1969), James Timberlake, *Prohibition and the Progressive Movement* (Cambridge, Mass., 1963), and Herbert Asbury, *The Great Illusion: An Informal History of Prohibition* (Garden City, N.Y., 1950), are three of the better books on the prohibition experiment. Biographical studies of champions of the fundamentalist crusade are William G. McLoughlin, *Billy Sunday Was His Real Name* (Chicago, 1955), Lawrence W. Levine, *Defender of the Faith, William Jennings Bryan: The Last Decade, 1915–1925* (New York, 1965), Aimee Semple McPherson, *The Story of My Life* (Hollywood, California, 1951), William G. McLoughlin, "Aimee Semple McPherson," *Journal of Popular Culture,* I (Winter, 1967), 193–217, and—the most recent study of Sister Aimee—Lately Thomas, *Storming Heaven* (New York, 1970). On the Klan, John M. Mecklin, *The Ku Klux Klan: A Study of the American Mind* (New York, 1924), David M. Chalmers, *Hooded Americanism: The First Century of the Ku Klux Klan* (New York, 1965), Kenneth T. Jackson, *The Ku Klux Klan in the City, 1915–1930* (New York, 1967), and Charles C. Alexander, *The Ku Klux Klan in the Southwest* (Lexington, Ky., 1965), are all penetrating accounts.

The political conservatism of the period is ably discussed by Robert K. Murray, *Red Scare: A Study in National Hysteria, 1919–1920* (Minneapolis, 1955), Stanley Coben, *A. Mitchell Palmer: Politician* (New York, 1963), and David Felix, *Protest: Sacco–Venzetti and the Intellectuals* (Bloomington, Ind., 1965). The immigrant question emerges from John Higham, *Strangers in the Land: Patterns of American Nativism, 1860–1925* (New Brunswick, N.J., 1955), and William Preston, Jr., *Aliens and Dissenters: Federal Suppression of Radicals, 1903–1933* (Cambridge, Mass., 1963). Other aspects of the conservative backlash are reviewed in Allen Guttmann, *The Conservative Tradition in America* (New York, 1967), Don S. Kirschner, *City and Coun-*

try: Rural Responses to Urbanization in the 1920's (Westport, Conn., 1970), and Keith Sward, *The Legend of Henry Ford* (New York, 1948).

Morrell Heald, "Business Thought in the Twenties: Social Responsibility," *American Quarterly,* XIII (Summer, 1961), 126–139, is an interesting contrast to Prothro, *The Dollar Decade,* while Kenneth A. Yellis, "Prosperity's Child: Some Thoughts on the Flapper," *American Quarterly,* XXI (Spring, 1969), 44–64, is exceptionally valuable for the student of social history. Albert Parry, *Garrets and Pretenders: A History of Bohemianism in America* (rev. ed., New York, 1960), is a significant study of American bohemian cults, as is Emily Hahn, *Romantic Rebels; An Informal History of Bohemianism in America* (Boston, 1967), although the latter becomes highly personalized.

A superlative account of the foremost hero of the decade is Walter S. Ross, *The Last Hero: Charles A. Lindbergh* (New York, 1968). An interesting volume for young readers is Rex Lardner, *Ten Heroes of the Twenties* (New York, 1966). The incongruities of frontier individualism in urban society are discussed with great insight by Walter Prescott Webb in *The Great Frontier* (rev. ed., Austin, 1964), while Ronald L. Davis, "All the New Vibrations: Romanticism in Twentieth-Century America," *Southwest Review,* LIV (Summer, 1969), 256–270, offers an explanation for the forces of rebellion growing in the United States since World War I and the need for redefining individual identity.

Among the best narratives of the expatriates are Malcolm Cowley, *Exile's Return: A Narrative of Ideas* (New York, 1934), and Matthew Josephson, *Life among the Surrealists* (New York, 1962), while R. P. Blackmur, "The American Literary Expatriate," in David F. Bowers, ed., *Foreign Influences in American Life* (Princeton, N.J., 1944), is a distinguished analysis. Howard Mumford Jones, *The Bright Medusa* (Urbana, Ill., 1952), shares a viewpoint similar to Bernard DeVoto's, while Alfred Kazin, *On Native Ground: An Interpretation of Modern American Prose Literature* (New York, 1942), is a classic study of recent American letters, a considerable portion of which is devoted to the 1920s. Valuable interpretations may be found in John Killinger, *Hemingway and the Dead Gods: A Study in Existentialism* (Lexington, Ky., 1960), and Frederick J. Hoffman, *Freudianism and the Literary Mind* (Baton Rouge, La., 1945).

Noteworthy individual studies of writers of the 1920s include John Malcolm Brinnin, *The Third Rose: Gertrude Stein and Her World* (Boston, 1959), Frederick J. Hoffman, *Gertrude Stein* (Minneapolis, 1961), Carlos Baker, *Ernest Hemingway: A Life Story* (New York, 1969), Robert Sklar, *F. Scott Fitzgerald, the Last Laöcoon* (New York, 1967), Andrew Turnbull, *Scott Fitzgerald* (New York, 1962), Arthur Mizener, *The Far Side of Paradise: A Biography of F. Scott Fitzgerald* (Boston, 1951), Arthur and Barbara Gelb, *O 'Neill* (New York, 1962), John Gassner, *Eugene O'Neill* (Minneapolis, 1965), Charles Angoff, *H. L. Mencken, A Portrait from Memory* (New York, 1956), William Manchester, *Disturber of the Peace: The Life of H. L. Mencken* (New York, 1951), Mark Schorer, *Sinclair Lewis: An American Life* (New York, 1961), and Karl W. Detzer, *Carl Sandburg: A Study in Personality* (New York, 1941).

The outstanding volume on the art of the 1920s is Milton W. Brown, *American Painting from the Armory Show to the Depression* (Princeton, N.J., 1955). Of the broad surveys of American painting Oliver O. Larkin, *Art and Life in America* (rev. ed., New York, 1960), and Edgar P. Richardson, *Painting in America* (New York, 1956), are among the best, both containing sections on the 1920s. An especially good chapter on the decade may be found in Barbara Rose, *American Art since 1900* (New York, 1967), rich in illustrations and solid interpretation. A perceptive general history of American architecture is Wayne Andrews, *Architecture, Ambition, and Americans* (New York, 1964), basically viewing the subject as social history.

Of the books on jazz the recommended comprehensive histories are Marshall Stearns, *The Story of Jazz* (New York, 1962), and Barry Ulanov, *A History of Jazz in America* (New York, 1952). Rudi Blesh, *Shining Trumpets:*

A History of Jazz (rev. ed., New York, 1958), contains an interesting thesis, essentially that jazz must be improvised and "hot" and therefore ended in Chicago. A sterling article is Chadwick Hansen's, "Social Influences on Jazz Style: Chicago, 1920–30," *American Quarterly*, XII (Winter, 1960), 493–507. The best overall treatment of music in the United States is Gilbert Chase, *America's Music* (rev. ed., New York, 1966), although the volume is stronger on art composition than jazz. Wilfrid Mellers, *Music in a New Found Land* (New York, 1965), is an interesting account by an Englishman, if the reader has some technical knowledge of music. Two of the better biographies of American composers who made their mark on the 1920s are Julia Smith, *Aaron Copland* (New York, 1955), and David Ewen, *A Journey to Greatness* (New York, 1956), the latter the story of George Gershwin. Audience reaction to an essentially European art form in the nativistic 1920s is discussed in Ronald L. Davis, *Opera in Chicago: A Social and Cultural History, 1850–1965* (New York, 1966), while the career of an American artist who enjoyed her major success abroad is recounted by Walter Terry, *Isadora Duncan: Her Life, Her Art, Her Legacy* (New York, 1964).

The evolution of Broadway musical drama, which made significant strides in the decade, is most intelligently described in Cecil Smith, *Musical Comedy in America* (New York, 1950), Stanley Green, *The World of Musical Comedy* (New York, 1960), and David Ewen, *The Story of America's Musical Theater* (rev. ed., Philadelphia, 1968). David Ewen, *The Life and Death of Tin Pan Alley* (New York, 1964), is an engaging narrative of American popular music, while George Eells, *The Life That Late He Led* (New York, 1967), is a nostalgic biography of Cole Porter, in some regards a musical embodiment of the 1920s.

Gilbert Seldes, *The Seven Lively Arts* (rev. ed., New York, 1957), remains one of the most incisive studies of popular amusements in the United States. A concise history of the development of motion pictures is Arthur Knight, *The Liveliest Art* (New York, 1957), including a particularly strong section on the 1920s. Also worth consulting on the growth of the American film industry are Richard Griffith and Arthur Mayer, *The Movies* (New York, 1957), and Lewis Jacobs, *The Rise of the American Film* (New York, 1939). Ben Hall, *The Best Remaining Seats: The Story of the Golden Age of the Movie Palace* (New York, 1961), traces with elaborate pictures how the motion picture became acceptable to the American middle class.

As the 1920s has been called the "Golden Age of Sports," John R. Tunis, *The American Way in Sport* (New York, 1958), adds a dimension to the popular culture of the decade, while John Tebbel, *George Horace Lorimer and the Saturday Evening Post* (Garden City, N.Y., 1948), probes another facet.

Outstanding unpublished dissertations on the cultural life of the 1920s include Warren I. Susman, "Pilgrimage to Paris: The Backgrounds of American Expatriation, 1920–1934" (University of Wisconsin, 1957), Arthur C. Ketels, "The American Drama of the Twenties: A Critical Revaluation" (Northwestern University, 1960), Chadwick Hansen, "The Age of Jazz: A Study of Jazz in Its Cultural Context" (University of Minnesota, 1956), and Benjamin M. Jeffery, "The *Saturday Evening Post* Short Story in the 1920's" (University of Texas, 1966).

Berkshire Studies in Minority History

Under the General Editorship of
Moses Rischin, *San Francisco State College*

Professor Rischin, author of *The Promised City,* nominee for the Pulitzer Prize, received his doctorate at Harvard University. He has been a Guggenheim Fellow, an ACLS Fellow, and a Fulbright Lecturer in American History. He has taught at UCLA, Uppsala University, and Brandeis University. He is author of *The American Gospel of Success* and *Our Own Kind.*

CONCENTRATION CAMPS USA: JAPANESE AMERICANS AND WORLD WAR II

by Roger Daniels,
State University of New York at Fredonia

This volume offers the first treatment by a professional historian of the social, political, and military aspects of the Japanese-American evacuation. Using a combination of regional and archival materials, the author analyzes both the persecutors and the victims and relates this special instance of persecution to the entire fabric of American racism. This *Berkshire Study* shows how undemocratic decisions can be made in a democratic society.
September 1971 / 244 pages / $3.50 paper

Berkshire Studies in American History

Under the General Editorship of
Robert E. Burke,
University of Washington

Professor Burke received his Ph.D. at the University of California, Berkeley. He is managing editor of the *Pacific Northwest Quarterly* and general editor of the *American Library* reprint series (University of Washington Press). He is author of several books, including *Olson's New Deal for California, The American Nation,* Fourth Edition (co-author), *The Federal Union,* Fourth Edition (co-author), and *A History of American Democracy,* Third Edition (co-author).

TOTALITARIANISM AND AMERICAN SOCIAL THOUGHT

by Robert A. Skotheim,
University of Colorado

The broad concern of this book is with the changing climates of opinion in the United States between the early 1900's and the 1970's. The essays included are concerned with certain assumptions, methods, and value judgments in the social thought of some of the intellectuals who expressed characteristics of the changing climates of opinion. The author attempts to indicate the relevance of the idea of totalitarianism, integral to the history of modern American social thought, to these assumptions, methods, and value judgments. A brief bibliographical essay appears at the end of this *Berkshire Study.*
September 1971 / 144 pages / $3.00 paper

Note: The *Berkshire Studies* described above are only two of many volumes to come in each series.

BERKSHIRE
STUDIES IN
HISTORY

Robert Allen Skotheim

Totalitarianism
and American
Social Thought